What readers h
Remembering You. ~.,~ ~~j~,~ ~,,,~

"Your book extends the frontiers of knowledge of human development. It should be must reading for everyone who is active in counseling."
Nancy Bender, Ph.D.,
Psychologist in private practice

"The section on learning to communicate with your unborn infant is beautiful. Thank you!"
Francis Andrews,
Mother of two children

"As an obstetrical nurse, I've always worried about infants feeling alone and unwanted in incubators. Your accounts have both surprised and pleased me."
Michelle McCall, Obstetrical Nurse, county hospital

"Thanks for the experience of reading this book! It brought to the foreground my own experiences with you - my prenatal regression was enormously healing and freeing."
Anna Arends, MFCC, Therapist in private practice

"After reading *Voices From the Womb*, I understood, for the first time, that the fears I have long held were a response to my prenatal experience."
Hugh Edwards, Account Executive, brokerage service

"The descriptions of making the transition from nonphysical to physical are riveting!"
George Johnson, Electrical Engineer, computer firm

"In spite of material success, I have always felt that this earth is an alien place to me. I was really excited to learn that I'm not alone with this feeling, and there is a logical explanation for it."
Sandra Kirk, District Sales Manager, software company

"I learned more about my feelings from this book than from four and one-half years of therapy."

Stephen Falcowski, V.P. of Marketing, insurance company

"Amazing! The accounts of how it feels to grow inside of the womb are simply fascinating!"

Evan Carroll, Ph.D., Research Biologist

"As an expectant father, I was particularly struck by the role a father can play while the infant is still in the womb."

Larry Thornton, Counselor, adolescent group home

"Your book has shed real light on my life. Before reading it, I thought my uncomfortableness in being male was solely due to me. Now I see that my mother was deeply involved."

Thomas Nakamura, M.A., College Instructor, adult education

"I have always had a difficult relationship with my son. This book helped me realize we had a conflict long before he was born. I wasn't ready to accept having a child until after his birth."

Wilma Vander Hoven, Realtor

"I cannot suggest a finer start to becoming a parent than your chapter recommending that we communicate with our unborn infant."

Frank Nunez, D.C., Chiropractor

Remembering Your Life Before Birth

by Michael Gabriel, M.A.

with Marie Gabriel, M.P.A.

Aslan Publishing
3356 Coffey Lane
Santa Rosa, CA 95403

Published by
Aslan Publishing
3356 Coffey Lane
Santa Rosa, CA 95403
(707) 542-5400

For a free catalog of our other titles,
or to order more copies of this book
please call (800) 275-2606.

Inquiries about speaking engagements
and private sessions may be directed to
Michael Gabriel, P.O. Box 8030, San Jose CA 95155-8030.

Library of Congress Cataloging-in-Publication Data:

Gabriel, Michael 1927
    [Voices from the womb]
Remembering your life before birth /by Michael Gabriel, with Marie
Gabriel.
        p.   cm.
    Previously published under title: Voices from the womb. With revised
introd.
    Includes bibliographical references: p.
    ISBN 0-944031-60-9 : $9.95
    1. Hypnotic age regression--Therapeutic use--Case studies.
2. Prenatal influences. I. Gabriel, Marie 1956– .   II. Title.
RC499.H96G33 1995
616.89'14--dc20
                                            94-37985
                                            CIP

Copyright © 1992, 1995 Michael Gabriel

Cover design by Sheryl Karas
Text design by Brenda Plowman and Joanne Flanagan
Printed in USA
First Edition

10 9 8 7 6 5 4 3 2 1

Dedication

To my daughter Celina.

In memory of my son, Geda,
And my younger brother, Sol.

To my clients,
who have shared their lives
and deepest experiences with me,
and whose courage and momentum
toward wholeness are so endearing.

Table of Contents

Acknowledgments

To acknowledge the assistance of others in bringing this book into print is to recognize the power of good will and personal affection. We are grateful to the following persons who have seen us through the composition and publishing of this book.

Hal Bennett, author, agent, editor, and guardian angel of this book. Hal guided us through a hitherto unknown journey, bringing our manuscript into print as a book. He reviewed and edited the book. His vision and creativity are much appreciated. His personal qualities and abilities have added a positive note to our lives.

Colin Ingram, whose line by line editing contributed immeasurably to our book. He is a writer with a dramatic flair and a creative imagination. His devotion to writing and his discipline contributed a steadiness to the entire project.

Edith Fiore, psychologist and author, whose kind and knowledgeable presence in our community strengthens the network of those who seek to better the human condition.

Dawson Church and Brenda Plowman of Aslan Publishing. We appreciate not only their acceptance of our manuscript, but also their assistance, strenuous efforts, and intention, as publishers, to provide books that will be of significant benefit to readers.

Author's Notes

The modern English language, despite its great richness and diversity, has some awkward aspects. Should we refer to an unborn infant whose gender is undefined as *he, she,* or *it?* Most commonly the unborn infant would be referred to as *he* or *it.* We decided, however, that the unborn infant should be recognized as present in both male and female genders, so we chose to alternate between the use of *he* and *she* in succeeding chapters.

The verbatim transcripts of prenatal regressions sessions that appear in this book have, in some cases, been edited for clarity and to eliminate redundancy. Furthermore, I have protected my clients' privacy by changing their names and, in some cases, obscuring their identities, while remaining true to the material we covered in our sessions together.

Disclaimer

This book is sold with the understanding that the subject matter covered herein is of a general nature and does not constitute medical or therapeutic advice for any specific condition. Anyone planning to take action based upon information provided by this book should first seek such professional advice as would be appropriate for his or her given circumstances.

INTRODUCTION

A Personal Note

My work has convinced me that our awareness begins much further back than psychologists had once believed, and that human consciousness extends beyond the limits of the five senses and brain. This book is a chronicle of exploration into new frontiers of our human experience.

—MICHAEL GABRIEL

Prenatal regression work explained the mystery of my own childhood. Before doing this work, what I consciously knew about my parents' early years in America was rather limited. They were Russian immigrants who had somehow ended up in a Brooklyn apartment house in the 1920s. My father spent long hours in his small grocery; my mother raised two sons, my younger brother, Sol, and me.

I remember a feeling of disharmony in my house. Not that there were fierce arguments or overt bitterness, but there was no warmth or unity either. My father complained a lot, often finding fault with my mother, and mother seemed distant and emotionally hard to reach. Because my parents were immigrants, they were not able to understand their Americanized children very well, and so the sense of separation was heightened.

The feeling of not being close, of not belonging, stayed with me. I grew up alienated from the people around me and from society in general. It was not pleasant, but I hardly knew what I was lacking. I only knew that I felt alone, without support, living in an unfriendly world. When I was in my late twenties, I escaped to California and had very little contact with members of my family from then on.

As an adult, I attributed my feelings of loneliness and isolation to childhood experiences. But about fifteen years ago, my memories were dramatically awakened by going through a prenatal regression while under hypnosis, and I was able to see that my feelings of disharmony went much further back than I had ever imagined.

When regressed to my first months in the womb, I vividly experienced my mother's feelings—a deep loss and pain. She was mourning. But there was a great mystery around all this. Who was it that had died? In the regression I sensed that Mother sorrowed for a man who had loved her deeply. So many questions came to the fore: Who was this man? How could I possibly know of such things? And why had my mother married my father, when she was still in such deep mourning for another man?

As I continued the regression I became aware of other significant events. In the first few months of my mother's pregnancy, my father repeatedly tried to reach out to her, but her grief overwhelmed her, and she was unable to respond. By the end of the pregnancy, a pattern had begun: my father frustrated, bitter, and complaining because his wife was never "present" for him; my mother apart, sad, and never able to resolve the loss of the man she loved.

Her pregnancy intensified my mother's sorrow over the unexpected death of her first husband, the man with whom she had dreamed of raising children. How was she to claim the infant she was now carrying? Mother's grief prevented her from bonding with her unborn child. Her feelings were intensely felt by the infant in her womb—me—and I now understood the source of my own feelings of isolation!

In the beginning I thought it possible that I was only imagining all these things. It didn't seem logical that I could know so much, that I could "share" feelings my mother had experienced before I was born. But a few months later, my regression experiences were verified. I placed a long-distance call to my brother, something I did rarely. We fought a lot as children and had never grown close. Now adults, we had not seen each other for thirty years. Perhaps it was a premonition on my part that had brought me to contact him, for he died unexpectedly a few months later. At the end of our conversation, almost by chance, I asked him if he knew anything about a relationship mother might have had before her marriage. Yes, he replied, Father had revealed a secret to him years earlier. After Mother emigrated to America, her childhood sweetheart came to join her. They were recently married and living in Minneapolis, he said, when her young husband slipped off a tall grain elevator and plunged to his death.

In the 1920s, a young widow—especially a recent immigrant—was in a precarious position, and remaining single was not a very practical option. My mother's sister hastily arranged a marriage for her to my father. And so it was that I learned of my mother's terrible grief, and her inability to be a loving wife to my father. The story of how my father and mother came together explained the family disharmony and confirmed the accuracy of my prenatal memories. *My feelings of separation had begun in the womb.*

It was this experience that helped convince me that the regression process I'd gone through was valid. I was motivated to incorporate prenatal regression work into my professional practice, so that I might assist others through this valuable process of reliving life's earliest experiences.

As you will find in the pages ahead, my clients have made exciting discoveries through prenatal regression work. As a hypnotherapist and intuitive counselor, my work is focussed upon the problems that my clients confront in their brave efforts to create lives of wholeness and joy. Nearly all of us see patterns in our lives that cause us pain and difficulty. In my own case, I lived isolated and apart from others without a sense of belonging; others have struggled with difficulties in relationships, poor self-esteem, the inability to keep a job, harsh self-criticism, or fears and anxieties that nearly consumed them.

Searching for the cause of these patterns often leads us to examine our childhood experiences. Sometimes these do provide the answers. Yet childhood experiences often only echo patterns of experience that started much earlier. The periods of infancy, birth, and the nine months in the womb that precede birth, frequently reveal intense core experiences—experiences that fuel our emotional responses to life. Until we do go back and resolve these emotional experiences, we may continue to live our lives like puppets controlled by the invisible strings of a forgotten past.

Understanding the Prenatal Infant

In the womb, the world we live in is very different from the one we know as adults. It is a world that most of us no longer enter, much to our loss. Our beauty and profound innocence are matched by an equally profound vulnerability. Here we live through our very first life experiences—and they become as much a part of us as the food we assimilate. To understand ourselves now, we must understand our primal life experiences. And to understand why these experiences made such an impression, we must understand the unique nature of the prenatal infant.

Although we do not have the power of speech in the womb, we are acutely aware. We feel the emotions of our parents, siblings and others. We sense biological events in our mother's body. We interpret and react to these feelings and events in ways often unsuspected, sometimes dramatic, and frequently surprising.

You can get a sense of the unborn infant's universe by watching young infants. They are so amazingly open and responsive to the environment. They live in a whirlpool of stimuli, of sounds, sights, feelings and energies all mixed together. They shift with the tide of competing energies, changing moods in an instant.

We are no less responsive to the environment as infants in the womb, but there the total environment is our mother. As unborn infants, we are enfolded within her body, we are "at one" with her. We do not have a sense of ourselves as separate, distinct individuals. We tend to empathetically absorb mother's, and occasionally father's, emotions without distinguishing them from our own. In the womb, we have no way to distance ourselves or escape from emotions that we find unpleasant or threatening. Perhaps more than at any later time in our lives, we are vulnerable. As adults, we have learned ways to be safe, but as prenatal infants we did not know these ways.

In the womb we have no barrier to the emotional forces of life. Our experiences may well be more intense before birth than at any later time in life. If we are to understand ourselves, our motives and personal development, the study of our prenatal experiences is invaluable. These experiences profoundly affect our ability to love ourselves and others and to achieve what we desire in life. My intention in writing this book is to demonstrate just how critical these experiences were—and still remain—and why this journey to the past provides a key to our liberation.

(For an eight-point summary describing the prenatal condition, see Appendix A: The Nature and Functioning of the Prenatal Infant.)

Adaptations in the Womb

How do unborn infants deal with the intense and affecting environment of the womb? A significant question! They adjust by making adaptations to the conditions they encounter, conditions which range from nurturing to intolerably harsh. The adaptations made are critical, for they set the life patterns that will develop after birth. They determine how infants will relate to their parents, siblings, and others. They determine basic attitudes about life. And they underlie the psychology of the adult.

Only deeply affecting experiences or devoted self-examination will ordinarily change these patterns. So it is not surprising that clients who come to see me are still living out their prenatal adaptations—ways of functioning that enabled them to deal with stressful conditions, but that are now detrimental to their lives as adults.

The case studies presented in this book answer many questions about how unborn infants cope when they do not receive emotional nurturing from their mothers. How do the unborn react when parents are in distress? What causes them to favor one parent over the other? How do they compensate for being unwanted or of an unwanted gender? Can they choose to be born early or to not be born alive? This book shows the varied ways in which infants have rescued themselves in trying situations.

(For a delineation of prenatal adaptations, please refer to Appendix B: Psychological Adaptations During Gestation.)

Healing the Child Within

As you read the transcripts in this book, you will read of events that have caused pain, fear, confusion, and even shock.

Feelings and adaptations that are no longer useful, and that are frequently even detrimental, can be healed through the process of "unhooking" ourselves from the past.

As a therapist, I work with adult clients to help them release the harmful emotions and attitudes stemming from their experiences in the womb. The wounds of the past, though hidden, continue to live on. In that sense, the prenatal self is very much alive within many of my adult clients. Releasing the past is critical if we are to respond with joy to the present.

I use four processes to heal prenatal stress and trauma. Were you to go though these processes with me, you would first enter into a deeply relaxed or hypnotic state, and then progress through them: **1. Recall:** you observe and give words to your prebirth experiences. **2. Reframing:** you bring objective adult perspectives to your prenatal experience in order to more fully understand what happened. **3. Releasing:** you let go of the emotions that were absorbed during the prebirth state. **4. Rescripting:** you use active imagination and mental imagery to relive prebirth experiences and key events since then. Positive images are imprinted in your mind and positive experiences in your feelings.

(For a more more complete description of therapeutic processes used in prenatal regression therapy, see Appendix C: Processes for Releasing Prenatal Stress and Trauma. This material will be particularly useful if you want to have insight into how to heal your own past, or if you are a professional therapist wishing to develop new modalities of healing.)

How Adults Relive Their Prenatal Experience

As we explore prenatal regression in the chapters ahead, keep in mind that this work has an important purpose: to free us from the ties and limitations that bind us.

The regressions are valuable, for they enable us to articulate feelings that previously were unrecognized and undefined. When we go back to our experiences in the womb, we use adult skills to sort out what happened to us at that time. Powerful experiences are brought to light that had been buried for so long. We gain a deeper understanding of the origin of our present feelings, and by doing so, we are able to release detrimental emotions which have limited and harmed us even as adults.

When we revisit prenatal life through hypnosis, we do not have exactly the same experience we had many years earlier when in the womb. For now we are able to recognize and define intense instinctual reactions that the unborn infant could not. We can understand what happened then. We "process" these experiences using our mind. But what we actually experienced in the womb were nameless responses to a variety of affecting emotions and energies.

Let me provide an example of how this works. An unborn infant who is unwanted will feel the charged emotions of the mother directed against him. He will then have a body response to these unpleasant emotions, and react away from the mother's feelings of anger or disgust which encompass him. Through repetition, his reaction will be reinforced. Finally the infant will emotionally withdraw from the mother completely, pushing away from her.

The response of a prenatal infant is comparable to the response of a child. If a parent yells at a child, his entire body may cringe as though he had been struck, though no physical violence had been committed. Later, the child may adapt to the experience by becoming rebellious or submissive. The prenatal infant, characteristically, responds on a primal body level.

An adult who regresses to the prenatal experience of being unwanted by his mother will say, "I made the decision to reject my mother." But this "decision" was originally made without the mind and without words. It was a body response to the emotional energies of the mother. When you read the transcripts of this book, what you will actually read are the body reactions of a prenatal infant translated into words by the adult.

The transcripts, chronicles of the vivid experiences of prenatal infants, expand our understanding of human development and of our soul journey. They pose many important questions for all of us. For example, if our consciousness begins before we emerge from our mothers' bodies, how far back does it go? Is it possible to have memories from early in our gestation? Is there some part of human consciousness that allows us to be aware of experiences at the time of conception or even before that? And, are memories valid when they describe experiences outside of physical existence?

The transcripts you read in this book may influence your opinion. My own work has convinced me that our awareness of this lifetime extends much further back than psychologists have traditionally believed, and that human consciousness is not limited to, or totally dependent upon, the physical apparatus of our brain and five senses.

A Vision of Possibilities

I have hypnotically regressed thousands of adults to their life in the womb. For fifteen years, I have listened to the fear, the anger, the joy and the love of unborn infants. My clients have been able to describe events that took place while they were in the womb, and during and following birth. Their recall of these experiences has been far from vague; it has been clear, vivid, and charged with emotional intensity.

If it is true that our memories extend back into life before birth, and perhaps even during and prior to conception, we are presented with a new set of responsibilities as parents and as a society. The knowledge gained through the prenatal recall process will, I believe, inevitably lead society to a new and loftier view of carrying, growing, and birthing a child. We recognize that we can start nurturing and supporting our children while they are still in the womb. Even in our earliest thoughts of the baby-to-be, before there are even the subtlest stirrings within the womb, we can send our children messages of caring and love to encourage them as they come into being.

As author of this book, I would like to state that it is not intended to promote a particular stand on the complex issue of abortion. I recognize that this book may be utilized by either side in this debate, and, like other prenatal investigators, I do not take a negative stand on the issue of choice. It is my primary intention that this book contribute much-needed insights into the situation that is really being debated, the embodiment of an enduring soul. Understanding this process enables us to go beyond the perspectives that have contributed to the conflict.

It is my desire to assist human beings in their quest to find inner peace and wholeness. With this in mind, I have included processes to assist my readers. In chapter 16, I provide precesses to enable the pregnant mother and father to better communicate and bond with the unborn child. In this chapter I also provide a process for those planning to have an abortion, or who have had an abortion, in order to bring about resolution and harmony—through communication with the soul of the unborn being involved.

For those of us in the helping professions, and for those who simply want to broaden their understanding of the events that have helped shape their lives, a new means of exploration is at hand. Through prenatal recall, deep and meaningful formative experiences come to light. We have a way to lift the burden of negative feelings and attitudes whose origins were previously unknown. As a consequence, lives can be transformed and uplifted.

It is my sincere wish that this book will succeed in bringing a message of hope and renewal. The transcripts that follow tell of a courageous venture into life. As you read these intimate accounts and share these experiences, perhaps they will prove as great a revelation and inspiration for you as they have been for me.

M.G.
San Jose, California
January 1995

1

No Welcome Given

Arnold: "I was living in her fear."

Many times when I address audiences or discuss the process of prenatal recall with new clients, I am asked: "What proof do we have that prenatal memories are real or that infants who are still in the womb are responsive to their experiences?" To answer that, put yourself in the position of a detective investigating a crime. Although you may not have observed a particular person actually committing that crime you do find evidence indicating that the person was in a position to do so. With a little more probing, evidence mounts, your doubt vanishes, and in the light of this mounting evidence the suspect ultimately breaks down and confesses.

While this is less than a perfect analogy, it is true that there is a certain amount of detective work involved in prenatal therapy, and this work produces evidence that ultimately leads to the validation of the prenatal experience. For example, something recalled in a prenatal therapy session may appear to explain why the adult client has panic attacks or uncomfortable psycho-physical symptoms such as asthma. The client works through the memory of the traumatic event that occurred before she was born, and following this the symptoms—which she has had since she was a tiny child—miraculously disappear, never to return. Later, medical records or conversations with older relatives, friends, or the parents themselves reveal not only that the event recalled was real but that there was no way the client could have known of that event except by experiencing it prior to birth.

As I sat down to write this first chapter, and to offer evidence of the kind I've described above, I remembered my work with a particular client, whom I'll call Arnold. Because his story deals with medical and psychological problems that could be understood in the light of prenatal experience, and because it reveals some of the benefits we can all expect to enjoy from this kind of work, I'd like to share his story with you.

The therapy session had been very revealing. Arnold's recall of life in the womb had been clear and explicit. But as we approached his birth, he suddenly began to gasp and breathe in short rapid breaths. His features looked strained, his fists clenched the chair. I watched him carefully because of the intensity of his reaction. I said to him, "Tell me what is happening. What do you feel?"

I'm panicking, I'm panicking! It feels real tight here, real tight and uncomfortable.

"What is happening? Are you trying to push out?"

I can't get the air in! (His body sagged, arms dropping to his sides.) I'm coming out, just going with it. The muscles are pushing on me...so hard, so hard. They are pushing me out. The muscles are overwhelming...I feel all locked in. I can't do anything...

It's like I'm on a voyage. There's this urge to start breathing as I go on, and I try to start breathing, but there is no way I can! As I come out, there is bright light everywhere, but I still can't breathe!

"Try to stay with it, just try to stay with it. Are you afraid?"

I'm trying to suck in with all my might. I try, try, but there's nothing coming in. I'm going to die! I think I am going to die! Now I'm coming out. I have to breathe, I'm trying to breathe, but there's still no air. Now I'm upside-down...I don't know...no, now my head is up. He (the doctor) sticks something down my throat. I'm choking, then there is relief. I...I start to breathe! I can breathe! (Arnold breathed in deeply, looking exhausted from his ordeal.)

They give me to my mother. I feel warmth. I'm wrapped up in something and close with my mother. I can feel her joy and I'm responding to that. It's warm, there's breath, there's light, there's closeness. I'm relaxing now, relaxing. Feeling her protection.

What has been extraordinary to me in these prenatal recall sessions is that virtually every client who goes through the process is able to recapture experiences prior to birth. It is not, I find, a matter of laboring to recall vague memories. On the contrary, often there is great clarity and a charge of emotion which is longing to be expressed, which is seeking to be translated into language and released. Are these intense feelings and memories mere adult fantasies of what prenatal experiences are like? In Arnold's case a little detective work uncovered some very interesting facts:

Arnold's medical records revealed that, at birth, he had been unable to breathe due to mucous in his nose and throat. The attending doctor suctioned off the mucus immediately, but the effect was long-lasting. During his early childhood, Arnold was repeatedly treated for severe asthma.*

---

*"Many specific birth experiences can lay the foundation for a chronic asthma condition later: temporarily drowning in amniotic fluid is one; having the oxygen supply cut off by a twisted umbilical cord is another; being too drugged to take that first breath outside the canal, still another."

—Arthur Janov, Ph.D. *Imprints*, p.83.

Arnold is a tall man. His face is a little like an eagle's, with his long nose and high forehead. He is personable and generally admired by others. A high school counselor, an aggressive amateur athlete, a responsible husband, and the father of two children, he compulsively strives to do his best at all times. Yet, as far back as he can remember he has been beleaguered by anxiety and a sense of isolation. And although he is in exceptionally good health, he has an irrational fear of health problems. He takes minor pains to be serious problems, sure that a life-threatening disease is just around the corner.

> If I'm having some kind of physical symptom, whether it's a pressure in my chest or an acid stomach...whatever it is, I automatically kick into extreme worry, fearing that something is radically wrong with me.

Arnold went on to explain that ever since he could remember, his anxiety escalated into total fear and panic.

> I remember being in college, away from home, lying in bed, listening to the radio, trying to fall asleep, and I would actually feel my adrenaline running from fear. I couldn't identify exactly what I was afraid of, but I would lay there with my heart beating, completely freaked out.

Tracing his feelings back to earlier years, Arnold remembered that as a child he would awaken at night and panic if the room was too dark. He explained that, even now, he "loses it" if he is in unfamiliar surroundings. He feels isolated, terribly alone, even though he is married and has a loving family.

We had begun Arnold's therapy session by exploring his central feelings of fear and insecurity. I had given Arnold some general instructions: "Close your eyes and relax. Now get in touch with your feeling of fear. When you've done that and you're ready to go on, just move your forefinger." After Arnold moved his finger, I told him: "Now maintain your feeling, and let's have you to go back to the origin of that feeling, wherever that may be. Just stay with that feeling." I had done nothing special to regress Arnold, no extended induction, but after a short time he responded by telling me: "It seems to be in the womb." What follows are excerpts of the actual transcript of Arnold's prenatal regression, as recorded that day.

Arnold's Recall of Life in the Womb

M: I would like you to tell me how it feels to be in the womb, after leaving the place you were in before.

A: *There is a real mood change. I'm no longer in a place that is light and free and easy - it's kind of darkish and empty here. It's comfortable enough for me, but there's been a definite shift from light and free and breezy to just kind of darkish. A definite change.*

M: Let's move forward.

A: *[pause, then] Tension...crying...stress...*

M: Who's tense?

A: *The surrounding. Whatever I'm in. The [amniotic] sac.*

M: How long have you been there?

A: *I don't know. I've got a feeling of having a body.*

M: What is the feeling surrounding you?

A: *Tenseness.*

M: Let's get a sense of how your mother's feeling.

A: *Upset.*

M: Why is that?

A: *She's pregnant.*

M: She's not happy to be pregnant?

A: *No. She's newly married. But her ties to her own parents are strong. They are having financial problems and they need her to assist in the store.*

M: She feels obligated to help them?

A: *Yes, she's been working in her father's business, helping him out, doing her family duty. Times are rough and they need all the help they can get. Her mother is angry at her for being pregnant, and acts as though her duty to her father should come first.*

M: And how does your mother feel about that?

A: *My mother feels a lot of guilt. She feels that she should be helping her family, that it is wrong for her to be pregnant. She believes she has no right to do this to her family! Right now I'm experiencing her physical reaction of tenseness. I'm feeling physically what she's going through.*

M: Try to get a sense of her relationship to her husband.

A: *She loves him. But she feels torn between him and her responsibility to her father. Her husband is on one side giving her advice, her mother's on the other side giving her just the opposite advice, and she's feeling guilty, trying to do the right thing.*

M: So both are giving different advice.

A: *Yes. Her husband thinks it's a good idea to have a baby. His reaction is "Great, we're having a baby!" But her mother says "No, it's selfish, it's wrong, you're hurting your father." She's feeling all of that and worrying. She's trying to resolve it and feeling very frustrated. She's upset and guilty.*

M: So what does she do?

A: *There's nothing she can do! She is pregnant, yet she wants to fulfill her family obligation and she can't do that. She just feels a lot of stress.*

M: And how does that affect you?

A: *Now I'm feeling that stress. I am feeling all her mind chatter, saying "I'm guilty, it's wrong—no, it's right." I can feel her emotional roller coaster, back and forth.*

   At first all this upheaval was outside of me, it was happening to the sac I was in. But now it is becoming part of me. I'm accepting it now as mine, as my feelings.

M: So then, what are your feelings?

A: *My mother's feelings are coming through me. Feelings of insecurity, of not being sure, of not being able to make a decision, like an overload. Should I be here? I am questioning whether I should be here or not. Is this all a mistake? I'm feeling pretty insecure, having some real doubts and I'm becoming frightened. I've gone from that warm feeling to feeling doubtful about what's going on. I feel real tight in my chest. It's not panic, just a lot of questioning. The security and warmth are gone. I was okay before this happened...I could just be here. Now I'm not sure. I have doubts.*

M: How deeply does that go?

A: *I've gone from okay to doubt, questioning. The feelings that were there before, of being connected, of warmth, of all that, all those feelings have been forced out of me. What is taking their place is darkness and emptiness, and a dreadful feeling. I'm taking in everything around me. Those feelings she has are mine. That's who I am. Negative feelings are replacing the positive ones.*

Prenatal Chronology

We then moved from the general feeling of the womb to a month-by-month examination of his gestation.

M: What do you experience during the first month?

A: *Just being here. My mother doesn't know that she is pregnant.*

M: What happens when she finds out?

A: *Shock, fear, crying—a trauma. But it feels outside of me, separate from me. There is tension but it seems apart from me, it doesn't seem like it has anything to do with me.*

M: Let's move ahead, a month later.

A: *The tension becomes more consistent. Tight.*

M: How is that affecting you?

A: *I am starting to absorb it, as if that's the way it is here.*

M: Okay. Now move to the third month.

A: *Upset...Both of us are upset. Sick. She gets sick, morning sickness.*

M: And how does that affect you?

A: *I am feeling nauseous, feeling like she does. Just ill.*

M: It must be pretty hard for you.

A: *It's not comfortable.*

M: And then what are you doing about it?

A: *Just going through it, like this is the way it is.*

M: Let's go into the fourth month.

A: *It's the same stuff, it just doesn't let up. Constant uneasiness. It's always there. Tension or doubt. Whenever I had the feeling of having a body, that's when the tension started to build inside of me. I can't tell exactly when that was. Maybe the second or third month.*

M: What are you doing at this point (fourth month)?

A: *I'm just kind of absorbing it all. Things are just happening.*

M: Let's go to the fifth month.

A: *Everything feels dark and empty.*

M: Your mother's not focusing love and affection and attention in your direction, or is she?

A: *No. It's empty here. Things just keep getting worse.*

M: Are you able to stand it?

A: *Yes, but there's no light or joy or anything. I'm just alone. Feeling isolated.*

M: Is that hard to handle?

A: *Yes.*

M: But you're just letting yourself go along with it?

A: *I don't know what else to do!*

M: Let's move forward to the sixth month.

A: *I'm alone. Feeling desolation here. Cut off. Wanting to not be here. Just pitch black here.*

M: Is it getting to be too much for you?

A: *It's just always there, I don't know what to fight. It's like it's part of me. It is me. I'm just out here in this black, alone. The darkness continues to grow.*

M: You're having all these feelings. Are they coming from your mother?

A: *Yes, they came from my mother. These are the feelings that I'm having. I've just accepted my mother's feelings as mine. I'm feeling what she is feeling.*

M: Let's move you to the seventh month. Are those feelings still there?

A: *Yes...but there are some changes. There's some kind of acceptance. I don't know if I've accepted that this is the way things are or if my mother's accepted something. Maybe I've just accepted the isolation. There's an acceptance of something.*

   I'm feeling a reduction in the intensity. Things are not getting worse. It's still dark and alone. But there seems to be a relaxing of sorts.

   There's a feeling of acceptance at some level. I think it's my mother...She's decided she's having the baby regardless of what anyone else thinks! I think she's finally gotten okay with it. Which doesn't do me a whole lot of good. (humorless laughter)

M: Why is that?

A: *Because I'm stuck out here in black nothingness. I've already given up! She made that decision, but I'm cut off from everything, including her. I'm not part of that decision. I'm still feeling aloneness and devastation and blackness.*

M: Is that as much as her change affected you?

A: *Maybe it did affect me somewhat. I'm not in panic, I'm a bit more accepting of where I am.*

M: Do you feel your mother's love and excitement about having a baby?

A: *No, it doesn't click for me, other than to feel her acceptance of the situation of having a baby. But it doesn't change my feeling. I am off on my own tangent now, locked in. I feel a degree of relaxation—I've released some of the panic and accepted the emptiness. But I can't change the emptiness!*

M: So you seem to be keeping your mother's previous feelings. The pressure you've felt is released somewhat, but you don't switch the way she did?

A: *No, I don't. We're going two different ways now.*

M: Let's move ahead to the eighth month.

A: *She's accepted it, she's going to have the baby, she's becoming happy and light. But that doesn't penetrate to me. I can see her change but I can't get it. I've been left out here alone and I'm hurting. She's been able to change and I haven't.*

M: So she's probably sending some love and energy to you now, right?

A: *Yes, but I don't know where to put her feelings. I'm encased in emptiness. She's happy, but I'm alone. She's made the turn and I haven't. I got left behind. There's light out there but I'm trapped in darkness.*

M: You're going the old way and she's going the new way. How is she with your father?

A: *Good. She's ending up looking down his path.*

M: So I assume he's happy. And then where are you with him?

A: *I have no real connection with him.*

M: Let's go forward to the ninth month.

A: *It's about the same.*

M: So you remain separate there in your mother's womb, separate from mother and father. They're having one experience, you're having another.

A: *Yes. Around the seventh month she made a turn and I didn't.*

M: How has that affected you?

A: *Those feelings of black isolation made it difficult for me to connect with others.*

As we proceeded, Arnold went on to describe his traumatic birth experience. After the regression ended, he appeared to be stunned. Before long, he was able to speak. "It's devastating going back to that feeling. I feel drained. It's not a whole lot of fun!"

In a session following the regression, Arnold had a number of insights about his prenatal experience. He recognized that his mother had felt an extreme fright and nervousness upon discovering that she was pregnant. He described her condition vividly:

> *It's like her blood was draining from her head and the fear was just running up and down her body. She didn't know what to do. She had the feeling in the pit of her stomach that she'd done something wrong, that she would now have to face her mother. She dreaded doing that.*

Arnold had apparently absorbed his mother's emotions. He stated, "I was living in her fear. I grew up in fear." He said that the fear continued right into adulthood. He would at times suddenly become panicked without knowing the reason. He had an irrational fear of illness. For all of his life, Arnold had felt an inner darkness and distress for which he could give no reason. He was now able to understand the prenatal origin of these feelings:

> *From her standpoint, my mother was thinking "I'm pregnant, but I don't want to be pregnant. I don't want to face my mother over this." But I took it personally, like she was saying to me "I don't want you." It's like her rejection of me was blaring over the loud speaker.*
>
> *I had nothing. I had no connection. It was cut off. And there was just a total sinking into darkness. That started the feeling of being alone, and it just grew from there. At the core of me was a terrible blackness that nothing could change.*
>
> *I felt so dark, empty, and unwanted during the prenatal*

period. I think that's what produced that deep feeling of empti-
ness I have now.

That seems to be the key, the decision of my life, the decision
that my mother didn't want me. That's been the guiding feeling
of my life.

After examining many transcripts similar to the one above, it becomes increasingly difficult to dismiss what clients report in these sessions as merely imaginary journeys created by a lifetime of learned facts, youthful memories of overheard conversations, or pure speculation. The correlations between the prenatal experience and emotional or physical symptoms are indeed convincing.

For there to be a direct connection between the symptoms and events occurring in Arnold's world prior to his birth and during the time he was in the womb, we would have to assume that our consciousness comes into being long before our brains have matured, as was thought to be the case until the last decade. While it seems unlikely that consciousness could somehow be separate from the brain and the five senses, there is evidence suggesting that this is so. In the next chapter we explore an interesting case which poses some dramatic questions about the beginnings of consciousness.

2

How Conscious Is an Unborn Infant?

Adam: "There's nothing to feel guilty about. I got to be here."

Adam was a small man with a wary manner and a sharp tongue. At the time of our sessions he was fifty-seven years old, and had lived all his life with a deep distrust of others. When we probed deeply into his childhood, we found a similar feeling, already entrenched, but no obvious experience that might have triggered it. I regressed him back through his nine month prenatal experience, but there was still nothing until we uncovered the moment of conception. Here is the significant excerpt from Adam's regression.

The Wrong Father

M: Let's move back to the first month. What are you feeling now?

A: *Something's wrong. It feels like they did something weird...like they feel guilty.*

M: What do they feel guilty about?

A: *[There's a pause for almost a minute, then:] I'm not sure....My mother feels as though something is not quite right, as though the pattern is not right.*

M: How does your father feel?

A: He feels inadequate, as though he is a failure as a husband.

M: And how do their feelings affect you?

A: Things don't feel quite right....It has to do with my being here.

M: They don't feel good about having a child?

A: They want to have a child, but there is a sense of wrongness. My mother is angry at her husband. She had to do something she didn't like because in some way he was inadequate.

M: What do you mean?

A: [There's a long pause, then:] I am getting the sense....It was a plan...they got someone else to donate sperm.

M: Can you describe the plan?

A: I can get it clearer now. My mother wanted a baby badly but she hadn't conceived after a number of years of marriage. Someone donated sperm. My mother inserted the sperm with her fingers... she didn't like doing that. But she did get pregnant.

M: And how do they feel about what they have done?

A: They are pleased they can tell everyone they will have a baby. And my mother likes being pregnant. But...[pause]

M: But what?

A: They are ashamed at the same time. They are trying to cover up their feelings. Nothing shows on the outside, but they both feel like they have sinned. It's weighing on them, like a dark cloud over everything.

M: So there is not a feeling of joy and love?

A: No. They did not consider how this would affect their relationship. My mother feels that she has sinned and that God will punish her. She always does what's right. Somehow she feels used.

M: Is she angry at your father?

A: Yes. He should have been able to do it!

M: And how does your father feel?

A: He fears he is not all he should be as a man. He does not claim me as his child.

M: And how do your parents' feelings affect you?

A: *It is all my fault! If I wasn't here, they wouldn't be having these problems. At other times, I am angry at them, picking up what is happening and reacting—at what a price to me!*

Following the regression, Adam reflected on some of the feelings he experienced after his birth:

After I was born they really loved me and tried to be good parents, but I was the result of their "sin." They never mentioned it to each other but neither of them could ever let go of it. I always felt that there was something wrong, something very wrong. It was there when I was growing up and it's always been there, but I never...I never imagined anything like this.

"How do you see your conception now?" I asked Adam. He responded:

"I feel like saying to them 'There's nothing to feel guilty about—I got to be here!' "

Emotions that Reach the Fetus

How remarkable it is that Adam could uncover secrets surrounding his conception and the reasons for the strange atmosphere of guilt and awkwardness that permeated his childhood. How can such awareness of the time of conception be possible? How can we register experiences that come about before our bodies were even formed? When do consciousness and memory begin?

These questions have been debated by increasing numbers of researchers and clinicians in recent years. Of course, the dominant position of medical science has held that, both prior to and immediately following birth, infants are unaware creatures whose brains are not well enough developed to record their experiences, and whose feelings are not significant. Perhaps because the cries of infants are not accompanied by words, such cries have been rather easily dismissed. And because prenatal memories, though powerfully affecting, usually remain unconscious, the cycle has continued unbroken: medical personnel and parents have treated the unborn and newly born infants the way they themselves had been treated—with very little sensitivity to their pain, emotions, and vulnerability.

But the past couple of decades have signalled change. Advances in medical technology have made possible much more detailed study of unborn and newly born infants. Doing what would have been considered impossible only fifty or one hundred years ago, scientists have been able to actually investigate the unborn infant while he is still in the womb. As a result, the physical, emotional, and cognitive development of the fetus have become less mysterious. We have a more complete understanding of how a mother's smoking, drinking, eating habits, and illnesses affect her unborn infant. Remember that as recently as thirty years ago, mother and fetus were seen as having quite "separate" biological systems. For example, pregnant women who practiced poor nutrition were assured that the fetus "took" from a mother what it needed nutritionally, in spite of her poor eating habits! We now know differently.

Even more intriguing are the studies on prenatal infants' personality development, learning abilities, and communication skills. A radically different picture of unborn infants has emerged. In his book, *The Secret Life of the Unborn Child*, Dr. Thomas Verny, a Canadian psychiatrist and leader in the prenatal psychology movement, states that "the unborn child is a feeling, remembering, aware being, and because he is, what happens to him—what happens to all of us—in the nine months between conception and birth molds and shapes personality, drives and ambitions in very important ways."

Knowing that unborn infants are "feeling, remembering, aware beings" leads us to a concern about our interactions with them while they are still in the womb. The psychologist Arthur Janov observes in his book *Imprints: The Lifelong Effects of the Birth Experience* that "Not only is the fetus affected by what the mother takes into her system—it is equally affected by the state of that system—is that pregnant mother easygoing, relaxed and calm; or is she chronically tense, depressed or agitated? Is her life situation quiet and stable or is she encountering crisis after crisis? Not so surprisingly, both animal and human research is showing how the mother's inner state profoundly affects the development and personality of her baby."

Modern researchers have given new perspectives on the theories and explorations of earlier theorists. Even without the benefit of current research technology, earlier investigators suggested that prenatal experiences were significant in human development. As far back as one hundred years ago, there was speculation about the trauma of birth and its subsequent effects on the personality. Even Freud entertained the idea, but ultimately rejected it and decided that his clients' birth memories were probably fantasies. However, one of Freud's disciples, Otto Rank, accepted birth trauma as real, caused by the infant's abrupt switch from the blissful, peaceful existence in the womb to the harsh realities of the outside world. According to Rank, birth trauma had far-reaching consequences in influencing adult behavior.

More recently, the possibility of trauma during gestation has been considered, as well. In the 1970s the psychologist Arthur Janov proposed the idea that "primal pain" was caused by traumas that were strongly imprinted but repressed, thus leaving adults with no conscious memory of them. Intrauterine and birth trauma were considered a significant source of primal pain. In his book Dr. Janov states, "Gestation and birth experiences can and do dictate how we act and react for the rest of our lives." Primal therapy, a method of "reliving" intrauterine and birth traumas, involved surrendering to the painful sensations and undoing the trauma by re-experiencing it.

Meanwhile, others were drawing conclusions similar to those reached by Dr. Janov about the significance of our earliest experiences. In 1971, psychologists and physicians in Europe established the International Society for the Study of Prenatal Psychology in order to promote the study and understanding of the unborn infant and the effects of womb experience. About ten years later, the Pre and Perinatal Psychology Association of North America (PPPANA) was established for the same purposes. One of the founders of PPPANA was Dr. Thomas Verny. His book, written in language that is easy for lay persons and prospective parents to understand, elucidates the research findings of the last decades regarding unborn infants and newborns. In print since 1981, this book has helped to bring about the needed shift in our perception of these very young human beings. His more recent book, *Nurturing Your Unborn Child,* provides prospective parents with a program of various processes designed to enhance the communication and bonding between parents and their unborn infant.

Another early member of PPPANA, the psychologist Dr. David Chamberlain, reports on how he was led to this area of investigation in his book *Babies Remember Birth:* "My clients kept telling me [under hypnotic regression], in considerable detail, what happened to them at birth, including the ideas they were having as babies. I found an unexpected maturity in their 'baby' thoughts. Each person spoke with authority and identity. They knew and loved their parents. Their character did not appear to be age-related or developmental in any simple sense; it was there from the start." Dr. Chamberlain's book reviews current scientific research and also presents clients' prenatal and birth memories.

The Czechoslovakian psychiatrist Stanislov Grof has done extensive research on birth trauma and prebirth states, originally with the use of LSD, and in recent years with non-drug "holo-tropic" breathwork. He is a leading thinker in the transpersonal psychology movement, which broadens the borders of traditional psychology to include spiritual perspectives and an expanded perception of the psyche. Dr. Grof's book, *Beyond the Brain: Birth, Death, and Transcendence in Psychotherapy*, discusses different stages of birth and their associated birth traumas. His research findings include reports going all the way back to conception. He states that "many subjects report vivid sequences on the cellular level of consciousness that seem to reflect their existence in the form of sperm and ovum at the time of conception."

Prenatal Infants Recall Their Experiences

The "memory" and "thinking" of prenatal infants differ from the way we adults think and remember. Obviously, infants do not have the mental abilities of the adult; they do not have a wide ranging, descriptive vocabulary, nor can they do complicated mathematical calculations. They do not register their experiences through a developed mind. (The same can be said for infants and young children.) Rather, as Janov states in *Imprints*, "fetal recall is a body memory. The body remembers, in its own way, and that stored 'knowledge' is no less valid than intellectual recall."

An argument commonly used to refute the idea of prenatal and birth recall is that the infant's brain is not developed enough to register experience. However, the fact that people do come forward with these memories suggests that either our understanding of the workings of the brain has been limited, or that we human beings have faculties for recording events that lie outside the channels of our rational minds and our senses. Dr. Verny reminds us, "The fact that we do not consciously recall something does not mean that it was not recorded. This, by the way, also applies to people under a general anesthetic. With the help of hypnosis, people who are hypnotizable remember with great clarity everything that was said and done during their operations...[there are also] well-documented cases of near-death experiences (see the writings of Kübler-Ross and others), where people who have been declared dead by their doctors return to life and report on every detail of what transpired in the room. They often know not only what was said but what was done to them, the expression on people's faces, what these people wore, and so on—things they could not have seen even if their eyes had been open—which they were not."

Going back to Adam's case at the beginning of this chapter, we find that Adam is reporting on a time when no fetus existed as yet, only the united sperm and egg. If Adam's knowledge of the conception and how it came about is valid, who or what is it that was conscious? Was Adam actually conscious before the moment of conception? If so, how long before that?

We may be able to find answers to these and other intriguing questions as we share more case histories of life before birth.

_3_

Coming into the Power
of Being Alive and Human

Judith: "When my mother is angry, that is what I am."

Growing a Body

When hypnotically regressed to the prenatal period, many of my clients are aware of their rapidly growing bodies. They are able to describe the physical changes they live through in the transition from being a fertilized egg to being a fully formed infant ready for birth. One client, Scott, described his experience like this:

> *I feel myself growing and changing—it feels strange and magical. I am forming and becoming* something. *Each time my cells multiply, I feel a rush of energy. I can feel my spine developing.*

During the third month, he said:

> *I feel an almost traumatic growth these first three months. I am coming into the power of being alive and human.*

Then a change came about. In describing his development during the fourth month, Scott said:

> *The bodily changes have slowed down somewhat. I can feel the umbilical cord, but I don't like it. I am not getting good nourish-*

43

*ment— it's almost like some poison coming in. There is nothing I
can do about it. I'm really uncomfortable.*

Concerned about this threatening condition, I directed Scott to
see what he was receiving through the umbilical cord, his life line
to the nourishment that sustained him. "Is there something wrong
with your mother's health?" I asked. I received an unexpected
reply:

*My mother is feeding me fear. I feel entrapped by it and I have no
way to escape. I'm stuck in her body and her fear— it's the only
way I can survive! As I grow bigger it becomes more difficult. She
keeps being afraid. She is having a hard time adapting to being
pregnant and is uncomfortable with not being in control of her
body.*

Scott's absorption of his mother's fear demonstrates how
closely his physical awareness and his emotional sensitivity were
connected. Later in the gestation, Scott grew more at ease. Describing his experience in the sixth month, he said, "I am stronger and
healthier and have grown a lot. I am restless to be born."

Another man, Allen, had a different way of describing the
feeling of growth:

*A vibration is surrounding me, an energy. It is erratic and rather
disturbing. I feel bursts of energy. Things are not in control. I see
bright lights of energy. I thought it would be dark in here but it is
light and somewhat comfortable. Things are going so fast, yet I
feel as though I am drugged, living in slow motion.*

Yet another client, Mike, was more specific. In the first month
of gestation, he said, "I am floating, feeling cushioned." He had
not yet identified with his physical body. Describing the next two
months, he said, "I am feeling more cramped and closed in, not as
full of spirit and life. The energy is getting stronger and stronger
now." By month four, he said, "I am heavier. My head is very

large." Reporting his experience in the fifth month, Mike noted, "My face feels misshapen or out of proportion. The upper part of my head is very large. I feel energy on my right side. There is more light than usual. I feel movement and have a sense of what is happening outside of my body—it's like hearing noises through a wall." Mike described the sixth month this way: "I feel a sensation in my chest or solar plexus, as though my awareness has moved to my solar plexus and dissipated from my head. I have more ability to move. The front of my face is filling in." Describing the final three months of the gestation, he gave this account:

Seventh month: *"My head is heavier and harder to control, but I am gaining a sense of my body. I am beginning to have an awareness of my upper arms and have more feeling in my back area."*

Eighth month: *"My head is still large but not as dominant. The rest of my body is developing, although it's still small in comparison to my head. I can feel my legs. I have a 'knot' in the area of my heart."*

Ninth month: *"I feel stronger. I have more sensations in my arms and legs, though not in my hands and fingers."*

Food, Tobacco, and Sex

The physical well-being of the unborn infant is critically dependent on the mother's physical condition, and it is affected by her habits and activities. What kind of life does she lead? Does she exercise and is she alive with energy? What about her smoking habits and her consumption of alcohol? An unborn infant is not only aware of her own bodily development, but is also conscious of the physical experiences of her mother, and is often strongly affected by them.

Food

In the third month of the pregnancy, one client strongly disapproved of her mother's eating habits: "If she ate better I would not bother her as much! Why is she eating pickles and ice cream? No wonder she gets sick, with that kind of food!" Not only did the prenatal infant know what her mother was eating, but she also had her own food preferences. Speaking of her mother's diet, she said emphatically: "I hate the sardines, but I love the chocolate!" (As fate would have it, she is now a nutritionist and gives advice regarding diet to her clients, telling them, no doubt, to eat *more* fish and *less* chocolate!)

In addition to noting food preferences, unborn infants commonly report on their mother's smoking, taking drugs, and indulging in alcohol. The feeling is often that of being poisoned, yet being totally helpless to do anything about it.

Tobacco

A study which confirms these reports about smoking was conducted by Dr. Michael Lieberman. Summarizing the findings, Dr. Verny writes that "an unborn child grows emotionally agitated (as measured by the quickening of his heartbeat) each time his mother thinks of having a cigarette. She doesn't even have to put it to her lips or light a match; just her idea of having a cigarette is enough to upset him....The fetus is intellectually sophisticated enough to associate the experience of smoking with the unpleasant sensation it produces in him. This is caused by the drop in his oxygen supply (smoking lowers the oxygen content of the maternal blood passing the placenta), which is physiologically harmful to him. But possibly even more harmful are the psychological effects of maternal smoking. It thrusts him into a chronic state of uncertainty and fear. He never knows when the unpleasant physical sensation will reoccur, or how painful it will be when it does, only that it will reoccur. And that's the kind of situation which does predispose toward a deep-seated, conditioned anxiety."

Sex

Are unborn infants aware of sexual activity between their parents? During regression, clients spontaneously comment on the sexual activity of their mothers and fathers—sometimes positively, sometimes negatively. Ned reported:

> *I know when they are having sex. I can tell then that they really love each other, and I feel like I'm a part of it.*

At the opposite pole, a client named Lizbeth said:

> *I am angry at my Dad. I feel his intrusion on my head. I am disgusted with my mother for allowing that intrusion. She should not be having sex at my expense!*

Another male client surprised me with his comments on his parents' sexual activity because his regression had begun so beautifully.

> *...I feel as though I am a cosmic spark coming into consciousness, an unbounded spark of life....[pause for one minute] Now I feel my entire existence threatened. I feel a jolt, a quick shift. My father is having sex with my mother. His penis is shaking the environment of the womb. It really disturbs me. I feel helpless and ignored, I can't fend for myself!*

Although it was early in the pregnancy and this unborn infant was not physically threatened by his parents having sex, he felt endangered. We later discovered emotional causes for these reactions.

Extreme effects of violent sexual activity late in a pregnancy were illustrated in a case presented at an American Psychiatric Association meeting. Reporting on this case, Dr. Verny wrote of "a man who was a severe chronic depressive who had never gotten along with his mother. An image he came up with under hypnosis was that of being pushed up and down in an elevator, which made him feel angry and depressed. He impulsively asked his mother whether she had sex during her pregnancy with him. She said yes, that her husband had forced himself upon her when he was drunk. Three hours later, her child was born."

Your Sorrows Are My Sorrows, Your Joys My Joys

We human beings are often emotionally propelled. By this I mean that we are strongly motivated by feelings and emotions, sometimes disguised under a veneer of reasonableness. Often critical emotional experiences early in life color the way we live our lives thereafter. They influence, among other things, the qualities of energy we express, the expectations we have of ourselves and others, our ability to succeed, and how well we relate to the opposite gender and to our own.

Despite the common stereotype that unborn infants, and even newborn children, are not really affected by their experiences, many prenatal reports show that they are extremely susceptible to the emotional climate in which they live. In fact, that susceptibility may be greater during the prenatal period than at any later time in life.

The unborn infant in the womb is completely encompassed by the emotional currents of the mother. Consider how sensitive most of us are to the emotions and feelings of those around us. We experience positive feelings of love and support, but also negative emotions of fear, anger, resentment, and envy—emotions that poison our atmosphere. As adults we seek out positive environments. The prenatal infant cannot. If life within the mother is oppressive, the unborn infant has no alternative place to go, no place of refuge or escape. Mother is the encompassing environment, the entire world in which they live.

In her prenatal regression, Judith was vulnerable to the instability of her parents and she absorbed their emotions. She described to me the impact of those emotions upon her when she entered the womb. She was strongly affected by them even though her parents were not aware of the pregnancy or of her existence.

> *I feel my mother's anger toward my father. I don't know what to do. I want them to love me—I don't know why there is argument. I don't feel okay. I cannot separate them from myself. When my mother is angry, that is what I am.*

Judith did not have a sense of her own separate identity. The emotions and feelings of her parents were so invasive that she could not distinguish their emotions from her own. Both her parents were frightened to discover the unanticipated pregnancy. In the womb, Judith responded this way:

> *I feel fear. Is it mine or not mine? It may be from them.*

Another client, Wallace, was able to identify his mother's emotions as outside of himself—but, nevertheless, the impact was similar:

> *She worries a lot and is unsure if she will be able to handle being pregnant. She lacks confidence. I feel insecure and am trying to adjust. Her feelings of fear are bigger than me. I am in the womb trapped in her feeling.*

Of course not only the negative emotions and feelings of the parents are felt by the developing infant. Love, warmth, the feeling of being wanted and nurtured are experienced with equal intensity. Regressed to the first months of his mother's pregnancy, Dan gave this happy report: "My mother wants me in a special way. She can hardly wait to see me, to find out if I am a boy or a girl. I feel a tremendous love from her— it's overpowering! It feels good and is expanding my heart." Another client reported a sense of wonderment and joy from her mother: "She drifts through the day touching her belly and feeling happy. I feel harmony between us, as though I am being welcomed."

Engulfed in Feeling, Unable to Discern

Unfortunately, the prenatal infant's extreme emotional sensitivity will sometimes cause her to see situations in a limited way or even to misinterpret them. One client, Ann, reported that her mother sensed that she was pregnant the moment that she conceived. Ann said of her reaction, "I don't think she likes it. It is an intrusion. She isn't ready to be pregnant. She is resistant and angry!" The reason was made clear when Ann realized that "she already knows that the marriage is in trouble. She is in a marriage that isn't working and now suddenly she becomes pregnant!"

Reliving the fifth month of pregnancy, Ann said, "I feel a sharp anger going to my solar plexus." Ann had taken in her mother's anger. But later in the regression session, Ann realized that she had completely misinterpreted what had happened. Ann explained: "My mother felt angry at her husband and I took it as though the anger was directed toward me!" Why had Ann not been able to distinguish that her mother was furious only at her father and not at her? It seems that Ann was unable to deal well with the emotion of anger, and had become overwhelmed by it. She had not been able to place herself outside the borders of her mother's emotion. She was within her mother's body and also within her emotional sphere.

Sam, another client, confronted a different parental conflict. Like Ann's mother, Sam's mother was angry, but not because she was pregnant—it was because she wasn't receiving enough attention from her husband. He, caught in his own professional commitments, felt guilty that he could not meet his wife's demands. In the sixth month of the gestation, Sam recognized that his parents' feelings were due to their own conflict, but he nevertheless assumed the blame for them. "I am the center of their bad feelings, the cause of their trouble. I don't feel good about myself." In order to deal with this, I instructed Sam to see the situation from the perspective of an objective observer. Sam said to me, "If I could have opened my eyes and seen their relationship, I could have adapted more easily. I didn't have the mind to go beyond my own hurt feelings."

A Loved Child's Dislike for Herself

Dora's story, which follows, is of interest to us here because it shows how a person can establish a sense of herself not as the result of particular life interactions but rather as a direct consequence of absorbing the mother's feelings during the prenatal period. We see how completely Dora did this:

D: *My mother has real doubts about life, wondering if it is worth being alive. She tremendously lacks self-worth. And yet she strongly wants to have this baby. She sends love to me but she can't love herself. I pick up on it. I don't differentiate between the love that's being sent and the self-hatred. The messages are intertwined. It's really hard to separate them.*

M: It's hard to separate the message she's sending you from the message she's sending herself?

D: *Yeah, I'm taking it all in. That message, 'I don't like myself,' the tension, all the negativity is absorbed by me directly. My mom is saying 'I am not okay' to herself. Because I'm inside her, I pick this up. She is me and I am her and I am not okay. I have no barriers. It's my message. It's me. I am not okay.*

I'm just absorbing everything from my mother on the physical level and the emotional level. Her self-hatred is just one more thing I'm absorbing. I don't even know it's bad. I have no ability to perceive if it's good or bad. It's just one more thing I'm picking up as I go along.

M: How does that affect you?

D: *It permeates everything! I have this core feeling of not being okay. It's base level—the knowledge is almost irrefutable. It's from my earliest consciousness. I am not okay.*

After the session, Dora recognized the significance of her prenatal experience and was able to articulate it very well: "That message [her mother's self-hatred] created in me an inability to fully accept love because I'm not feeling okay. It also made it harder for me to trust or love myself."

Stories such as Dora's make it so very clear that the prenatal infant's whole world, and her way of perceiving, is one of powerful receptivity and an inability to discriminate between self and other. It will be years before the self-identity and separate will have developed, along with the mental faculties for evaluating experiences.

In doing prenatal regression work, we see again and again that the unborn infant's responses to emotions and energies outside itself are kinesthetic. Even before the brain is able to interpret experiences, our bodies feel and record our joys and hurts. The body holds the record of all that we have experienced.

Enduring Consequences

In terms of personal and psychological development, how infants respond to their prenatal experiences has deep significance for them. The experience in the womb is not something that was left behind in the distant past—it has enduring consequences. Our prenatal responses become deeply ingrained and have a continuing impact. In the womb, we react from a limited perspective and we respond as well as we are able. We assume emotions and habits which define our personalities and set a direction for our lives.

Observing how we dealt with our prenatal experiences can unlock secrets about who we are now and how we live our lives.

Dr. Janov states that "The true knowledge and interpretation of early trauma—its unconscious meaning—comes with its total reliving. It is then that the deep-lying, motivating forces behind all later behavior are uncovered for the person, who will then have such insights as, 'I see now why I have despaired over the smallest setback'; 'I see why I've been so pathologically competitive—I needed to be ahead of everybody'; 'I've always felt battered by life, have been easily hurt, and now I know where the battered feeling comes from.' "

Going Forward

If we were forever locked into these early patterns that were set in place before we had the ability to question what we were experiencing, our lives would indeed be limited. We would truly be at the mercy of events over which we have no control. However, there can be no doubt that through the recall process and many other processes now available to us for personal development, our insights about our lives before birth can lead to adult understanding, a liberation from early negative experiences, and increased autonomy and freedom of choice.

In the following chapter I have attempted to paint a picture that reveals links between a mother's inner conflicts about her own self-worth and the self-worth her daughter later feels in adulthood.

4

No One to Rely on but Herself

Sandy: "I am trapped inside her body."

A hypnotherapist has an exciting occupation. No matter how many clients I have seen, I never know what the next person will be like, what qualities that special person will have, and how our work together will unfold. Sandy required some getting used to. From the moment she entered my office, Sandy stood out—a colorful woman. She wore bright scarves tied around her head, baggy pants and boots, and looked for all the world like a modern-day Gypsy. Sandy talked loudly, as though she were delivering an address to a large group without a microphone—and I was sitting in the front row! She was in her mid-thirties, and she had come because "my relationships with men are a mess!"

As we spoke, I sensed that she wasn't really happy with herself; she saw no reason why a man would want to be with her. Our first two meetings convinced me that Sandy's dislike of herself and her belief that she was undesirable to men had been established very early in her life. It seemed as though a regression might provide some answers, and so we began like this.

I instructed her to lie down and to become totally relaxed, releasing tension from her body with each exhalation of the breath. She did so, and we continued. "Visualize yourself in a peaceful and serene setting, a place that is special to you," I said. In that totally relaxed atmosphere, I had Sandy visualize herself lying down and falling into a deep and comfortable sleep. I then instructed her to allow herself to drift into a pleasant, dreamlike state. At that point she was deeply relaxed. Her mind put up no barrier. I then suggested that she move back in her memory to the time when her mother's pregnancy began. The string of memories began to unwind. I asked her to describe the first month in the womb. Suddenly, all relaxation left her body. She appeared stressed, her facial muscles taut. She spoke from her trance: "My stomach is tense. I am by myself. There is no one to help me."

We moved to the third month of her gestation, and Sandy's attention went right to her body. "I am curled up, warm, and floating. I want to keep my eyes closed and not think, and be warm. I am protecting myself. I just want to stay this way." She had a feeling of foreboding, saying, "I don't have a good feeling about what might be happening."

Proceeding to the fourth month, Sandy said:

> *I am real nervous. My mother is very apprehensive about the pregnancy. She doesn't know what will happen in her relationship with her husband. She doesn't know how he feels about the pregnancy. She doesn't believe what he says—that he still loves her.*
>
> *She is afraid that she will lose something. Her fear is that he will leave her and she regrets that she got pregnant. She doesn't think she can survive without his taking care of her. She doesn't understand him—he isn't that serious. He is a happy-go-lucky type and she is a serious type. She thinks he should take her more seriously.*

Her mother's doubts had a strong impact on Sandy: "I am so nervous. I feel impending doom. What will I do? I don't want to be left by myself."

Sandy clearly understood why her mother was so threatened by the pregnancy. She said, "My mother thinks she needs to be beautiful to keep her husband. She hates getting heavy with the pregnancy." But how did the husband feel about his wife? Sandy, encapsulated in the womb, was able to see how he felt more clearly than his own wife could! She said:

> *He is really excited about having a child. He loves her and cares about her, and he has a sense of responsibility toward her. But she doesn't register his feelings, she's too busy feeling sorry for herself. Instead, she thinks "Why is this happening to me?" She likes being a martyr. She is so afraid of not receiving love that she doesn't even see his love.*

In her description of the fifth month of the pregnancy, Sandy said, "I am worried about what will happen next. She doesn't like being pregnant. She feels trapped, as though she can't go places with her husband. She doesn't feel pretty." Sandy's next statement showed how strongly she was affected by her mother's emotional turmoil.

> *I threaten her survival. It's because of me that she thinks she is unattractive to her husband. She doesn't like me. I think it's something I did. I made a big mistake—if I could change, I would. I am growing and she doesn't want me. I am tense and lonely. I wish I could be somewhere else!*

It was clear that Sandy's mother had so much nervous energy and fear about the pregnancy that she didn't even know her own feeling about actually having the child. Aside from the fear of displeasing her husband, did she really want to be pregnant? How did she feel toward the infant in her womb? Her fear prevented her from reaching her true feelings. As the pregnancy continued, tensions escalated. The sixth month brought more conflict for Sandy's parents. Sandy reported:

My mother fears that she has lost her husband. They argue a lot. She thinks that no one likes her, especially my father's family. She just doesn't trust or believe him. My father leaves and returns; he is confused and upset. He doesn't understand why she is behaving this way.

Meanwhile Sandy felt like a victim: "I am stuck with her. I am trapped inside her body, trapped with all that nervous energy." The parental arguments evoked her fear: "I am afraid my father will go away, that my mother will cause it. I want to make it better, but I don't know how."

All this built up, causing an extreme reaction from Sandy in the eighth month:

I am getting angry. I kick hard and she passes out on the street. At least that starts her thinking! For the first time she is concerned about me. It gets her out of the reverie about her husband and into real awareness that she is pregnant.

But afterward she felt remorse and regretted her action: "I've felt guilty about that kick ever since."

How Sandy's Birth Was Affected

The tense, emotional situation continued into the last days of the gestation without any resolution. It affected her birth and the events following. Sandy said, "I resisted being born and was born three weeks late."

After the late birth, neither Sandy nor her mother seemed able to reconcile:

I rejected those things that nourished the body. I was born with an allergy to my mother's milk. She didn't nurse me. I was so angry I didn't want anything from her!

Sandy's resistance to nursing was shared by her mother. The young mother was confused about her baby. Sandy saw that "she doesn't want to nurse me because she would be too tied to me. She is fighting against feeling too close to me." Her mother's ever-present belief that being tied to her newborn would endanger her relationship with her husband was a barrier preventing her from developing an affectionate relationship with her own daughter.

Sandy's Adaptation: Self-Reliance

The effect of the prenatal experience continued on into Sandy's childhood. She felt separate from her parents, fending for herself. She exclaimed, "I was a passive brat! I was good at manipulation. I learned to manipulate by being what they wanted." Acting the way her parents wanted her to act, she was outwardly accommodating, but inwardly rebellious.

As an adult, Sandy carried the effect of her prenatal experiences embedded in her personality. The "unwanted" infant grew up to believe that others would not want to be in a relationship with her. Her sense of inferiority prevented her from developing satisfying relationships with men. Sandy's early life experiences taught her to rely only on herself. As an adult, she emphasized self-reliance. She ran her own boutique, unwilling to depend on or receive from others. As she herself said, "I assumed I could save myself. I wanted no help."

The Foundation

Physically naked and vulnerable, the infant in the womb is also emotionally naked. The experiences encountered there are all that this infant has known in this life, and they initiate his expectations about what life will bring. Because he will generalize about the nature of life on the basis of personal experience, the experiences in the womb take on a special significance. He will build a personality, a psychology, based on these experiences.

The views of the world that are developed in utero will most likely not even be consciously recognized later. And yet those views of the world could hardly be more significant, resulting as they do from intense, though hidden feelings. These core feelings are critically important, for they set the emotional atmosphere in which a person lives and through which a person looks at life. Dr. Verny states, "The womb, in a very real sense, establishes the child's expectations. If it has been a warm, loving environment, the child is likely to expect the outside world to be the same. This produces a predisposition toward trust, openness, extroversion and self-confidence....If that environment has been hostile, the child will anticipate that his new world will be equally uninviting. He will be predisposed toward suspiciousness, distrust and introversion. Relating to others will be hard, and so will self-assertion. Life will be more difficult for him than for a child who had a good womb experience."

So we see that the unborn infant, surrounded by love, nurtured, feeling wanted, will have every reason to expect that the natural order of life is supportive and that it provides an opportunity for self-expression and adventure. Contrast that with an unborn infant who feels unwanted in a friendless world. How likely this person will be to find life a hostile encounter, to dislike himself, to lack enthusiasm, or to anticipate that momentary happiness will surely give way to misfortune.

If you look perceptively at an adult, you can often recognize the child living within that adult. Certainly our reactions to others, or to life situations, are sometimes irrational, and we express the intense feelings of a child, untempered by the intellectual moderation of which an adult is capable. For the child lives within the adult as the base upon which the adult personality rests. An appropriate metaphor would be that of a house structured upon its foundation. We live in the rooms of the house itself, but it rests upon a base that determines the fundamental stability of the entire building. A poor foundation promotes the appearance of cracks and limits both the soundness of the structure and the height to which one may build. Though largely invisible, all depends upon the foundation's construction and strength.

The Body Does Not Forget

The body does not forget what eludes the mind. Who we are today is due, to a significant degree, to our experiences in the womb, and to the way each of us has responded to those experiences.

In our example in this chapter, Sandy felt herself to be unwanted and compensated for it with an excessive independence and self-reliance. In what other ways have we adapted our lives in reaction to our prenatal experiences? And what do we do with the knowledge gained through prenatal regression? These are some of the questions we will pursue as we continue together on this journey into the world of the unborn.

5

Assuming Responsibility
for the Parents

Katie: "My mission is to save their marriage."

My client Jason is a biochemist in his mid-forties. In contrast to flamboyant Sandy, I felt I needed a can opener to pry him open. Jason was intense and tightly controlled. He dressed with care and precision, and lived from his intellect while he sought to extinguish his emotions. When he uncovered his prenatal experiences, his personality structure began to make sense.

Sympathy Becomes Responsibility

Jason had a great deal of difficulty relaxing and was wary of anyone attempting to "control" him. We began with a series of simple exercises designed to ease his apprehension. For Jason, just feeling deeply relaxed was a new experience. Once he relaxed and was comfortable, we began a regression that took him back to the womb. In the first month of gestation, Jason reported that it was peaceful and pleasant in the womb. But then he sensed his mother becoming disturbed.

> *My mother feels a lot of love for my father, but there is nothing coming back! There is no warmth from him—just emptiness and*

63

coldness. She is in distress—she doesn't know why he has completely turned off his emotions. He is so cold—like ice! I feel sorry for my mother—she is insecure and rejected.

She doesn't know what to do with her deep feeling of love when he doesn't accept it.

It wasn't long before his mother began to protect herself.

She is backing off, not knowing what else to do. She slowly shuts off her feelings—I can feel her doing it! She shuts her heart, hiding her hurt.

Soon after his mother discovered that she was pregnant, the atmosphere became more highly charged.

I feel tense. My mother makes me tense. She just figured out that she is pregnant. There is a moment of panic. She wonders "Now what do I do?" I've been feeling good until now—but now she is not okay. She doesn't know what to do.

His mother's panic became understandable when Jason explained that his parents were unmarried. The pregnancy brought fear to his mother and guilt to his father. Bound to each other by these emotions, they remained together. Jason's father did marry his mother, but could not bring himself to do so until after Jason's birth. Jason said, "He is angry and frustrated with my mother, feeling an obligation to marry her. He feels he has no choice; he is forced to marry her."

How did Jason respond to his parents' discontent? Speaking of his mother's morning sickness, Jason said: "I feel guilty for having a bad effect on her health." Of her distress, he said, "I feel sorry for her. I feel responsible." Jason took his responsibility to heart, but he felt neglected.

Now I know why babies kick—for attention! I have the urge to let her know I want her attention, but I restrain myself—I don't kick. If I kicked her, she would think about me. But I don't want to disturb her! I don't want to intrude.

(In contrast, remember that Sandy, in the previous chapter, did kick her mother to get noticed—but felt guilty afterwards. Though Sandy used aggression and Jason used responsibility as coping tactics, both infants felt victimized.)

Jason spoke of his response to his mother's unhappiness: "This is all so hard for my mother. I need to help her make it through." As a child, he was exceptionally helpful and responsible, constantly attentive to his mother's needs. He did not draw close to his father. Jason remained angry at him for causing his mother pain, saying "he shouldn't have treated her that way."

Jason as a man is that same prenatal infant grown large. Responsibility is his middle name. Demanding of himself, he works many hours daily. But it is not only his job that he takes very seriously. Jason has a wife and three children. He tries so hard to be the responsible husband and father, to do what is "right"—and it is all this effort that makes him hard to live with. He tries to control everyone so that everything is perfect. But Jason's actions backfire. His children, longing for love, acceptance, and support, become angered by his efforts to control them.

Jason's prenatal decision was to take responsibility for relieving his mother's misery. Obviously, that was an impossible task for any infant. Even now, he is still trying to "save" others. The extremity of his efforts reflects the extremity of his prenatal experience. The emotional intensity of that trauma is still being lived out forty-six years later.

Why Infants Blame Themselves

Unborn infants confronted with an unhappy mother often respond as Jason did. They feel responsible for their mother's misery; they feel powerless and guilty because they are unable to alleviate it.

I have found that poor self-esteem is common among those infants who, like Jason, try to "rescue" their mother. They have a "body logic" that says: "I am here and mother is unhappy. If there is something wrong, it must somehow be my fault; and I am responsible for correcting it." If you analyze the situation, it doesn't really make sense that the infant is responsible. But the emotional atmosphere in the womb and the intense connection with the mother, combined with the infant's lack of mental discrimination, prompt the infant to take the blame. Her response is existential, not logical. The infant is at fault just by the very fact of being connected with her mother. Then, when she is unable to correct the problem, her self-esteem is further diminished, and self-blame and guilt accompany her failure.

The original problem usually results from the mother's poor self-image or the discordant relationship of husband and wife. Since the infant is not the real cause of the distress, she is not ordinarily able to resolve it. What a burden is lifted when an adult in regression finally recognizes that she was not at fault for her parents' unhappiness! With this realization, the flood of vital life energy that had been tied up is released and the person can more freely go forward, unhindered, in new directions.

Katie: Another Rescuer

Katie, a business manager in her thirties, took on a mission. She felt responsible for the well-being of her mother, as Jason did for his, but she took on a much more active and aggressive role in trying to rescue her. At the beginning of her regression, Katie described her existence in the womb:

> *It's dark, with little or no energy. I'm cold, trying to generate warmth. I was so excited to come, to have the chance to love and be loved. Now I am trying to figure out what is wrong. This will be harder than I thought.*

Katie spoke of her mother: "She is cold and clinical about having me; not excited and loving. She shows no feeling toward me." Nor was the mother better with her husband. Katie said:

She is not expressing herself with her husband. She is afraid of being vulnerable and blocks her feelings. When my father sends her love, what she does is she shuts down. She is disarming the person who loves her! She thinks she needs to keep strong, which to her means not feeling. All of her energy goes to maintaining herself and being in total control.

The marriage was already in trouble. Even so, Katie saw that her father was excited about his unborn child. She had a definite approach to the marital conflict: "I want to come out and convince my dad to stay." She took on the responsibility of keeping the family together.

How did Katie view her mother's lack of connection with her? Katie took the blame. She said:

It's very frustrating for me. I have an intense need for an intimate relationship with my mother, but I'm not getting it. I am not wanted or loved. I wonder what's wrong with me. There must be something wrong with me. [This in spite of the fact that Katie "knew" it was her mother's problem.]

In the face of this, Katie was very courageous. She said:

The less I get from my mother, the more I try. Inside myself I feel confused and unwanted. Outwardly, I feel I need to do something. I take on a mission. My mission is to save their marriage, to keep my father there. It's real exciting—I will save her marriage!

By the seventh month of the pregnancy, Katie's parents were still in disharmony. Feeling the emotional stress, Katie said:

It hurts in my solar plexus. My mother doesn't receive my father's love, so he pulls away and blames himself. It doesn't make sense. He hurts emotionally—but she sees him as weak. She will not allow weakness. In her anger, she is using me as a barrier against him.

Meanwhile, Katie once again bravely renewed her "mission":

I am real excited and feeling stronger. I can do something! If I can win my father over, he will stay. I can give him a reason to stay. Then both of us can put our energy into making Mother happy.

In Katie's regression, her birth was approaching.

M: What is the state of their marriage now?

K: *My father is feeling frustrated and rejected. My mother is still protecting herself by closing off from him.*

M: Katie, can you recognize what is going on with you?

K: *My energy is high, but it's a mask, or I wouldn't be able to go on. If I believe I can really help my parents, that helps me hide my hurt feelings. But behind it all, I don't feel wanted. I don't know what I am doing here. I feel desperate!*

The mission of saving her parents' marriage was Katie's protection against being an unwanted child. Those feelings were just too much for her to face.

Just before her birth, Katie reported that she wanted to "get out and get going." She said that her attitude had an effect on the delivery, assisting in making it rapid and relatively easy.

Mission Impossible

A child's best efforts are unlikely to rescue a marriage, despite the efforts and beliefs of that child. Katie, like Jason, was not able to recognize the limits of her effectiveness and responsibility. It was highly unlikely that she could have achieved her goal of saving the marriage. Her parents delayed, but separated a few years after Katie's birth. Katie said, "My father saw that the marriage wouldn't work, so he moved on. However, I didn't move on. I clutched the fear that I wasn't wanted." She remained tied to her mother, constantly attempting to please her.

Katie's situation was not altogether negative. During our sessions together, she learned that her mother did love her, but that her mother's fear blocked the expression of that love. Letting herself feel the depth of that love was, for Katie, an important step in healing her wounds.

The Defenseless Infant

Conflict between parents often has an extreme impact upon the unborn child. Adults may have many options by which to ease or resolve their discord. They can talk to one another or talk to friends; they can make love, take a vacation together (or apart), or they can seek professional assistance.

Completely surrounded by the emotional energy of the mother, the infant does not know how to remain neutral or objective. She has no choice but to live constantly affected by the emotional atmosphere in which she lives, and she is not able to escape for even a moment.

As Dr. Verny states, "An adult, and to a lesser degree a child, has had time to develop defenses and responses. He can soften or deflect the impact of experience. An unborn child cannot. What affects him does so directly. That's why maternal emotions etch themselves so deeply on his psyche and why their tug remains so powerful later in life."

The prenatal infant must then do something to deal with the surrounding energies, must make some adjustment to the situation. And the adjustment that is made is limited by the emotional resources of that infant.

The unborn infant feels with such intensity that there is often little objectivity in his actions. The threshold of what is tolerable is low. The connection with the mother is so intimate, and the sense of personal identity is so undeveloped, that she is likely to be deeply affected by the experiences that are going on around her.

She needs to find a way to deal with those circumstances, to adjust to the situation in which she finds herself. She needs to survive.

The adjustment that she makes has a powerful influence on her future. She develops a psychology that governs her future actions. Her response to a specific prenatal problem may become her general response to life problems, the automatic way in which she meets the challenges of life. Basic patterns of behavior are established in this way. Thus the realm of the possible has been established. In the womb she takes the first steps on the thousand-mile journey, steps that determine the direction which her life journey will take.

Therapy Brings New Awareness

In order to change unrewarding behavior, we therapists enable our clients to bring into clear consciousness those habitual responses that are self-defeating. When conscious awareness is brought to bear upon our unconscious and ingrained reactions, it is possible to release the self-destructive patterns and to seek out alternative, healthier, and more gratifying styles of life.

The prenatal infant can take on particular ways of functioning, of responding to life, and over time these become habitual. But the early habits that were established in the womb were unexamined and unevaluated. Later, even though the individual grew from infancy to adulthood, the habitual responses did not really change. The infantile moods and emotions were disguised, perhaps, but they continued to be highly influential. The therapeutic process allows responses that have been assumed without discrimination or thought to be reviewed, and more appropriate responses to be chosen.

Striving to Make Amends

Each marital relationship is as unique as the individuals involved, and each unborn infant is also unique. And yet prenatal responses fit into patterns. One of those patterns is the basic response we've seen in Jason and Katie's stories: the unborn infant takes the blame for the parents' unhappiness and then feels obligated to assist them. This may seem like an implausible response, for rarely is the conception of a baby the actual cause of the parents' unhappiness. And how would this diminutive infant be able to release their lifelong discontent and make them happy and content?

Questions such as these might be addressed to an adult, but not to a prenatal infant. The infant's emotional at-oneness, lack of discrimination, and lack of an identity separate from the mother's make these questions irrelevant. The feelings of the mother are experienced with immediacy and intensity. The sense of self as separate from the identity of the mother is slight, so that there is a close identification and empathy with the mother's emotions. Taking on the responsibility for the parents comes easily to these infants.

Courage Is Rewarded

The efforts made by Jason and Katie to assist their parents to live harmoniously didn't work. Their efforts did not unify the parents. And yet the efforts made did have positive results for these two individuals, for the courage and resolution they displayed as infants became parts of their character. Taking responsibility furthers the emerging identity of the unborn infant. Now that they have released the sorrows of their prenatal infancy through our work together, their fine qualities shine all the more.

Assuming responsibility is one pattern of response to prenatal stress. But there are other ways in which unborn infants respond.

The next chapter takes up a different kind of pattern, with different results.

6

A Retreat from Life

Steven: "I become disconnected,
withdrawing into isolation. I give up feeling."

"I am being pulled down to earth by a soft and gentle gravity. I am not sure that I want to do this. I don't know where it is taking me. I don't know what to expect." These were the first words of Steven's regression, but the gentleness of his entrance would contrast with his later experiences in the womb. Like Jason in the previous chapter, Steven had an unhappy mother. But where Jason assumed the blame for his mother's unhappiness and tried to help her, Steven reacted differently.

One of the most interesting aspects of doing regression work is discovering the unique response each unborn infant makes to the conditions of life within the womb. Two infants can live through relatively similar prenatal experiences, and yet have adjusted to those experiences in ways that could scarcely have been more dissimilar.

Why do infants react differently to comparable experiences? Siblings who have been born to the same parents and have lived in the same environment are sometimes radically different, and may have contrasting temperaments, personalities, and appearances. As often as not, brothers and sisters differ considerably in personal qualities and intelligence. These children are intrinsically different—different from the very outset of their lives.

Perhaps genetic makeup—our unique cellular imprint—creates these differences. Another possibility is that environmental differences, beginning with the environment in the womb, determine personality. It has also been suggested that the personality exists before the infant incarnates, that the character has been forged through the experiences of many past lives—a reincarnational approach. You can choose your own interpretation, but what is evident is that human beings are unique and distinct at the very start of life. My own work over many years confirms this fact. Each of us has a unique personality and a soul orientation that determine how we respond to experiences.

Steven

The first time I saw Steven was when he ambled quietly into my office. He was a man of fifty-two, and an accountant by profession. He had been married for about twenty years and was the father of three teenage children. He had come to see me because he felt pressured by three things in his life: he had been laid off from his most recent job and needed to make an important decision about his next career step; he had a feeling of distance from his three adolescent children and did not know how to relate well to them; and he was distressed by the constant bickering that had gone on for years with his wife. She, too, came for a few of the sessions, angry about her husband's detachment and his lack of emotional commitment. It was as though Steven had never assumed a commitment to his wife and family. And yet he had fulfilled all the outer responsibilities of a husband and father, and he had never been unfaithful to his wife.

We began by investigating Steven's sense of isolation. Yes, he felt alone despite the presence of his family. In fact, he had felt separated and isolated from others most of his life. Even as a child living with his mother and father he had felt that way. It seemed likely that prenatal regression therapy would uncover the reason for Steven's detachment from others. Seeking the answer, I guided Steven back to his earliest life experience.

A Journey into the Womb

He began by describing his experience of coming into the earth dimension: "I am being pulled down to earth by a soft and gentle gravity. I am not sure that I want to do this. I don't know where it is taking me. I don't know what to expect." During the first months of the gestation, Steven said, "I am 'in and out' several times." By that he meant that he alternated between inhabiting the physical body of the fetus and leaving it temporarily.

Reports of people leaving their bodies in the prebirth experience are similar to those reported by researchers of the near-death experience (NDE), the best known being Dr. Raymond Moody, author of *Life After Life*. Dr. Moody's book describes the experiences of patients who have technically died, left their bodies, and then returned to them. Many of these people describe an afterdeath journey into a dimension of peace where they were greeted by special beings and where they reviewed their lives. These reports also have a similarity to the OBE (out-of-body experiences) described by Robert Monroe, author of *Journeys Out of the Body*, and other researchers. Both studies indicate that consciousness is not confined to the body.

Steven continued, describing his initial experiences with his mother:

> *She is happy I am here. I am feeling my connection with her. I am flowing around the center of her being. I am expanding. I see a bright light in my mother's abdomen. It's the flow of energy associated with the pregnancy.*

Steven also felt a positive connection with his father, saying, "I have a deep sense of love for my father." His mother, however, felt quite uneasy about her husband. Steven said, "She is concerned about whether he is ready to have a child. She is not sure how he will respond when she tells him she is pregnant. She's anxious about telling him."

In the second month of her pregnancy, she got up her nerve and told him. Steven described his father's reaction:

> He explodes! He blames her for getting pregnant—how could she do this? He is frightened inside, unsure that he is up to being a father. He has a basic doubt about whether he will be able to handle the situation, and it comes out as anger.

Steven's mother was deeply affected by her husband's response. He reported, "She is shocked! She didn't expect such a strong reaction. She is afraid that he will hurt her. Her fear goes very deep." Steven explained why:

> She had been married to a different man for a short time before she married my father. In that marriage, her husband beat her, and she still has a fear of being physically harmed.

Like her husband, Steven's mother also expressed her fear through anger. She responded aggressively, verbally defending herself and attacking her husband. "She isn't even aware of her own forcefulness," Steven said. "Her attacks are powerful—they hurt my father just as his outburst hurt her."

Those attacks did not go unnoticed by the invisible observer, the unborn infant in the womb. Steven's reaction set the pattern for his life. He said, "I feel stunned by it, as though I am frozen in position. I become disconnected, withdrawing into isolation. I give up feeling." Steven did not blame himself and try to make things better for his parents, like Jason and Katie. Unlike them, he withdrew and disconnected himself from the emotional shock. His response was passive.

For the husband and wife, the course of the remaining seven months of the pregnancy was set as sure as clay hardening in a mold. Everything was an after effect of their painful argument. They pulled away from each other. Each blamed the other for the pain. In her distress and confusion, Steven's mother also withdrew from her emotional connection with the child in her womb; it was the pregnancy that had caused such hurt between her and her husband. She had been happy to be pregnant until the cataclysmic argument with her husband, but now Steven's mother shut herself off from her child.

The parents' emotional scars did not get healed after the birth of their baby boy. His parents separated and were divorced while Steven was still an infant. Nor did Steven's wounds get healed. From the second month in the womb through all his years of growing up, he felt isolated.

The hurt and isolated infant was still visible in Steven as an adult. His training as an accountant had strengthened his logical thinking, but he remained unable to express his feelings. That single dramatic confrontation between his parents had convinced him that emotions were threatening to his very existence, and he had shut down the feeling part of himself. So, for fifty-two years, he had never been emotionally close to anyone, living only in his mind.

The Consequences

We find all around us people who cannot live with their hurt, who cut themselves off from life. Infants like Steven become adults who feel beaten by life, who lack spirit and resilience. They have given up the fight. They are the victims of life, the victimized. They invite aggressive behavior; the bully instinctively picks on them, knowing they won't fight back. Others become frustrated and angered by their lack of response. In Steven's case, his wife reacted by taking charge of the family. She was dominant, he was excluded from forming a close connection with those he loved.

Resolving His Problem

The shocks of the prenatal period shaped Steven's personality, creating an emotionally withdrawn adult living life though his mind. Through our regression work, Steven was able to recall his prenatal experience and to understand the source of his isolation. Nevertheless, it took several sessions before he began to release the deeply embedded fear that had possessed him for fifty-two years.

Gradually, Steven accepted his parents' discord for what it was—the result of an incompatibility between his parents, and not due to him. This allowed his trauma to be lifted. In spite of their actions, Steven had loved his parents. The infant part of him—that lives on within Steven's adult personality—was now able to reestablish the love connection with his mother and his father. He could feel their underlying love for him. He could understand that their fear had disguised their love.

Steven, both infant and adult, began to change. He recognized the natural love he shared with others. He established a closer relationship with his own children, and he began to improve his relationship with his wife. He no longer had to be withdrawn and apart from others in order to feel safe.

An Unwilling Arrival

It is true that Steven had closed himself off from family and friends, but he had been fairly successful in his accounting profession. In contrast, from the first moment Bob walked into my office, he carried the air of a loser. He seemed almost apologetic. There are many reasons why clients entering a therapist's office for the first time may feel awkward. In Bob's case, I sensed it was a feeling of unworthiness—he acted as though he should not be intruding upon me, wasting my time.

Bob's prenatal difficulties had begun right at the very outset. As soon as he felt himself being pulled into life on earth, he said:

> *I am uncomfortable. I don't want to be here. I don't feel right. Somehow I am embarrassed—perhaps just being a child embarrasses me. I have been drawn to the earth plane but I'm not prepared. I felt a strong pull drawing me from a comfortable place, and I came, but I shouldn't have.*

What an inauspicious beginning! But Bob did manage well for a while. Describing the first two months of the gestation, he said, "It's warmer and cozier than before. I am a breathing, living thing. I feel myself growing and moving. It feels good." But by the fifth month, he began feeling highly uncomfortable:

> *I have a tenseness in my body. I want to leave! My mother has a stomach ache, maybe because I am pressing against her stomach, making her double over."*

I asked Bob how his mother was feeling toward him. He replied:

> *She is busy dealing with housework and is not attending to me. I just feel dragged along. My face feels red, flushed, and embarrassed. Maybe I don't belong here at all. I have the feeling I am feeding off another person when the person could be doing better things. I am an intrusion!*

Bob was showing his native disposition. He was uneasy and he felt guilty. He felt he didn't have the right to be distressing his mother by being present within her. He was also aware of his father's uncertainty.

> *My father doesn't know what to expect from my birth. My mother had one prior pregnancy that ended in miscarriage. So maybe he's concerned about that. I don't get a warm feeling from him.*

However, as happens in so many cases, the parents gradually became reconciled to the pregnancy and accepted the reality that a child would be coming into their lives. By the seventh month of the pregnancy, they were excited about the unborn infant. Bob reported:

> *They are giving me more attention. I get some love and awareness from each of them. My mother is feeling fulfilled. She is stroking her stomach, feeling the fullness and aliveness inside. My dad is smiling, looking forward to the birth.*

With a child or adult, receiving love generally causes a response in kind. But an unborn infant sometimes is unable to release the earlier emotions. And in this case, although his parents began to express more love toward him as excitement mounted about his birth, Bob did not change. During the regression, he said "I am still as disconnected from them as I was before."

What causes the prenatal infant to sometimes become locked into old emotions, unchanging and inflexible? Often it is the emotional impact of that earlier experience. Insecurity and fear have been absorbed into the fetal body, into the cells of the growing infant. Once set in place, they cannot easily be released, even though the original reason for them has disappeared.

Traumatic impressions tend to live on in both infants and adults. But these have a greater impact on the infant since he does not have a perspective on human behavior, nor a sense that conditions can change. In comforting a child, an adult will say "It will be all right," recognizing that the child lacks experience and does not readily understand that things change in time and he can feel safe again.

We continued the regression and Bob described his feelings as the end of the pregnancy approached:

> *I am becoming real claustrophobic. I feel a lot of anxiety; I am trapped! I can't move around! It's like being trapped in a place,*

not wanting to be there. Right now I feel physically nauseous. It's hard to breathe. It goes on and on and I cannot control it!

I asked Bob how his parents felt immediately before the birth. He replied:

My father feels a sense of fear and apprehension. The prior child miscarried. He is afraid that I will come out wrong. My mother feels a sense of fear, even of an emergency. They may have to rush to the hospital.

Then, describing his own discontent, Bob said:

I am so frustrated! I wonder what I am doing here. I can't stay here! Why am I here in the first place?

The actual birth process was difficult:

There is a lot of pain for my mother. She believed that the birth would be painful and that is what causes the difficulty. She does not relax until she is given an anesthetic.

I am sharing my mother's horror of the birth. I don't have any feelings except that I just want out of this confinement!

I come out without joyful anticipation. I feel like a stranger. I have a vision of walking up to my parents and shaking hands with them in a formal introduction, saying "Hi, I'm Bob, your new son," but I'm not sure how they will react.

Describing his condition immediately after the birth, Bob said:

I am lying on my stomach. I feel good to be free. I can breathe more freely and I am more relaxed. I am no longer confined to the womb, subject to those conditions.

Although he was relieved to be outside of the womb, Bob still had a difficult time facing life. Continuing the regression, he said:

It's not over. I have no right to be here. Now I have to deal with the outside world, with even more pressure of its own. The outside world is not safe, and I feel no basic security from my parents, no connection with my mother or my father. I need to protect myself.

Even now, Bob is resigned and without much fight. He still feels like an intruder, embarrassed just to be around others. His attitudes remain reminiscent of the time in the womb when he felt that he didn't belong and that he was imposing on his mother. Also, Bob feels cramped by physical circumstances, as though he lacks the freedom to do what he wants to do. He felt claustrophobic and trapped while in the womb, and he still has not released that feeling.

Infants Respond Individually

In the previous chapter, we saw how unborn infants assumed the blame for their parents' unhappiness and attempted to help them by taking responsibility for them. In this chapter, Steven and Bob, reacting in their own ways to their parents' unhappiness, withdrew from life in an attempt to protect themselves.

This defensive response can lead to despair. What a precarious situation the prenatal infant is in when he becomes separated in feeling and real personal connection from his parents! When this happens, the infant loses the connection that gives security and nurturance. In hurt and fear, the infant withdraws into isolation. Others become a threat to be guarded against. Instead of trusting others, the isolated infant seeks to be self-reliant. One does not have to search far to find this personality type.

Many of us are living such lives. We each walk our own pathway in search of wholeness. Surely, part of our path to completion and wholeness is back to our own beginnings, toward a deeper understanding of our earliest roots.

7

Some Choose Sides
And Some Choose Success

Bill: "I see my father as a rival"

A family I know has one son and one daughter. When they are out together, walking, they always walk in pairs—the mother next to her daughter and the father alongside his son. Occasionally they try changing partners. But, as with most efforts that go against a natural instinct, this doesn't work, and they revert to mother-daughter and father-son companionship. The boy, who is ten years old, very competitive and assertive, and not by any stretch of the imagination a "sissy," nevertheless always holds his father's hand when they stroll. It is a nice sight to watch them. The boy never does that with his mother. While mother and daughter are close, they do not have this kind of relationship.

The ten-year-old boy has "a big mouth." He mouths off a lot, just as his father did when he was young. So the two of them get into frequent fights and neither one gives in. But in spite of this, since the boy was born, he and his father have a kind of under-standing—a sense that they are pals. Pals are people whose friendship transcends trivial annoyances; they are close no matter what, and they will always be that way.

Of course, the flip side of child-parent affinity can mean that the child dislikes or is indifferent to the other parent. Such favoritism can begin early in life. Sometimes, the favoritism goes deeper than the natural affinity that children feel toward a particular parent. Children are sometimes emotionally open to one parent, but closed to the other. Our earliest memories reveal such biases. What causes a child to prefer one parent and, in some cases, to reject another? According to many prenatal regression reports, this situation may come about because of events that occurred during the gestation period.

A Decision Made in Anger: Rejecting Mother

Janice clearly favored her father over her mother. "I've never been close to my mother," she declared emphatically. "My father is the one who understands me."

Janice's interesting prenatal history revealed why she had always been antagonistic to her mother. She began by describing her discomfort at the beginning of the gestation.

"I feel very confined and dense. I don't like it here! It makes my stomach and head hurt to be here." Her mother was not any happier than Janice. Janice described her mother's feelings during the third month of the pregnancy with these words:

> She lives in her own fantasies. She feels life should be fun but she doesn't want responsibilities. The pregnancy is weighing on her, forcing her to face the fact that she is going to be responsible for another creature. She has never shared much with her husband, and she has lived until now just being concerned with her own needs.

Three months later, tension started to build:

> I feel caged in. The feeling I get from my mother is negative, dark, and gloomy. She is confused, not knowing what to do. I am a real disruption to her. She feels lost and so do I. I am unhappy that my

mother is not happy. I can't make her happy, so what good am I? I decide I am not worth anything.

And again, in the fifth month:

My mother is upset. She is resisting giving up her dreams. She had been spoiled and favored by her own father. And now she is angry at her husband and at me because we are destroying her fun. We have created a heavy burden in her life.

At the doctor's office one day, Janice's mother said "I don't want the baby!" That crucial declaration did not go unnoticed by the attentive prenatal infant. Janice said, "I hear her say she doesn't want me! I don't know who she said it to, maybe to the doctor. She keeps thinking it, too." It was all too much for the infant. After hearing her mother's statement Janice made a life-affecting decision. She cast off any sympathy for her mother.

I feel sad, then angry, at my mother. I'm tired of it all! She is dominating, a spoiled brat! She is afraid of responsibility and she never thinks about anyone but herself!

Janice could have absorbed her mother's emotions and taken blame for her mother's unhappiness, as we've seen with other unborn infants. But Janice responded in an entirely different way. She discarded her mother in order to maintain herself. It was an act of survival. Her sympathy for her mother was replaced by anger and rebellion. She decided to not be a victim, to not be subject to her mother's emotional weaknesses. So she separated herself emotionally from her mother.

Immediately following the birth, a common yet dramatic turnaround occurred. At the sight of her tiny baby, Janice's mother felt, for the first time, a profound maternal protectiveness toward her. She awakened to the reality and the wonder of having a child, and she felt so very badly for not having welcomed her child earlier. Her heart opened to her newborn infant with love and tenderness. The infant, however, did not respond, or relent. It was now too late. Janice said, "I have no tolerance for my mother. I detach from her and cut her off!"

Janice felt that she had to do it in order to survive. Emotional survival, to her, meant separation from her mother. She dared not trust her mother's expression of love, and she, as an infant, did not have the flexibility to change her attitude. The hurt she had felt from her mother was deeply embedded, and she could not let go of the past.

In the months following the birth, Janice's mother became aware of her daughter's unresponsiveness. And remembering how she had refused to accept her child during the months she had been pregnant, she tried even harder to make up for it. Thus, the childhood pattern was set—the mother trying to please the child, the child being pleased almost never!

In the year following her birth, Janice punished her mother. She said, "I always cried. Each time she came close I would cry." The pattern continued throughout Janice's childhood. She said:

> My mother tried to be kind, but I didn't want any part of it. When she tried to help me, I was very critical of her and would blame her. On my sixth birthday, my mother put out an enormous effort planning my birthday party. I complained about the way she prepared everything. After that experience, my mother swore she would never again give me a birthday party.

Throughout her life it had been that way: the mother seeking her daughter's approval and acceptance, and the daughter never giving recognition to her mother's affection.

Like Infant, Like Adult

All Janice's later friendships and relationships were affected by the attitudes that developed from those early experiences. As a child she focused her attention toward boys rather than girls. She was a tomboy herself. Her reaction away from her mother became generalized as a reaction away from females. She had no female friends. She emphasized those interests that have traditionally been associated with the male approach to life, especially success in business. She obtained a degree in business administration, and has moved ahead to become a successful executive. Her extreme efforts, coupled with natural organizational skills, have enabled her to succeed. She relates far better to the men in her organization than to the women.

Letting Go of the Past

Letting go of hurt was important if Janice was to change. By reliving her prenatal experience, Janice was able to better understand her mother. The key was to realize that her mother did always love her. The love was there—as it is in most cases—but it was suppressed by fear and insecurity. In one of her sessions, Janice said:

> *I became self-sufficient, setting up barriers to my mother. It was a sad decision! I lost connection with others. I set up barriers to separate myself from them. Now I am opening to other people, learning to be nurtured and feeling connected. It doesn't work to pull into myself anymore. I want to receive caring from people.*

Janice hardly dared open her heart to her mother, for she had closed her heart to protect herself. And daring and wanting are not, by themselves, enough to change an ingrained habit. It takes time, practice, and patience. But Janice has succeeded, and she has freed herself from the prenatal hurt that had such an impact on her life. She has taken up the challenge of becoming more loving and vulnerable with the same energy and zeal with which she pursued her career interests. When I see her now, my impression is of a warm, caring person who has her life well in hand. The change has been dramatic.

A Father's Prenatal Rival

In Janice's case, while she was in the womb her mother initiated the separation between them. In a different scenario, Bill felt separated from his father. But in this instance, the unborn infant initiated the separation rather than the parent.

As with several other husband-and-wife situations we've looked at, Bill's mother and father were in conflict over the pregnancy. His mother had wanted to bind her husband to her, and getting pregnant seemed like a good way to do that. The parents were young and recently married, and the decision to have a child had not been mutual. Bill's father was resentful. His wife had become pregnant in order to entrap him.

From his side, the husband was afraid of being tied down with a family, and apprehensive about the responsibility it entailed. More money would be needed, and he feared he could not earn it. So instead of binding her husband to her, Bill's mother had made the marriage even more shaky by becoming pregnant, and this added to her insecurity.

While this was going on, Bill, the central player in this drama, was in the womb unnoticed, struggling with the situation:

> *I feel isolated and don't feel good about myself. I am burdensome to my mother. Being in her body, I have a special sensitivity to her feelings, so her sadness and fear are with me each day. I want to help her. I decide that it is my function to make her happy.*

Bill's father was afraid, too, and he could be seen as the victim of a willful wife. So Bill could just as easily have taken his father's side. But this was not Bill's response. Rather, he was sympathetic to his mother only, and he went so far as to decide it was his responsibility to make her happy. When Bill decided to help his mother, he did so at the expense of his father. "I will be more considerate than my father," he said. "I want to be my mother's favorite. I see my father as a rival."

For a time Bill was effective. By sending his mother feelings of love and friendship, and feelings of distrust about his father, he adversely influenced his parents' relationship. By the fifth month the parents' conjugal relationship had became strained. Bill said, "I am getting in the way of their sexual relationship. Now my father feels jealous of me because of my connection with my mother." It was clear to the husband that his wife was directing her attention to the infant in the womb. The inhibited sexual interaction was an outer expression of the inner rivalry between Bill and his father.

But in this case, the couple's basic love for each other won out. As the pregnancy progressed, they reconciled, and a greater harmony developed between them. They were now looking forward to the pending birth. However, Bill did not change. He remarked:

> *I am still not feeling good. They are putting out energy toward me as a couple, but I don't receive it. They do want me now. My mother wants to give a real shot at being a mother, and my father also wants to be a father. His resentments are gone. But I still do not feel like a wanted child! I am not open down deep in myself.*

Bill didn't want to be born, but natural forces were in control, and he had no choice. Following the birth, both parents were excited. His father was especially happy to have a son. But Bill, the son, was unmoved. He reported:

> *There is no way I can love my father. He made my mother unhappy. I will go through the motions of being his son, but he will always be an enemy!*

Bill's father tried but was never able to close the gap between them. The emotional separation between father and son was detrimental to Bill as well. Although he had set himself up in rivalry with his father, he became the son who emotionally "lacked" a father. And so what was sown was reaped.

Now in his mid-thirties, Bill has created a life that is consistent with his prenatal decisions. The child who criticized his father for not supporting his mother took on the role of Superdad—the overly-responsible supporter and protector of his own family. Bill has become something of an extremist under the guise of being considerate and sensitive. He supports others, but doesn't recognize the support others might wish to give to him. He is an Atlas, holding up the world all by himself.

Bill was devastated by his divorce after eight years of marriage. All of his efforts to make his marriage succeed failed. In the womb, he had not "saved" his mother, and in his own marriage he had not "saved" his wife. Actually, neither wanted or needed saving. His sense of responsibility for them had limited his ability to have a relationship with them. He also strove to be protective of his son, to be the father that he had not allowed his own father to be. But the excessive concern for his child was not always conducive to his son's well-being.

Being forced into a divorce brought about a difficult and important transition for Bill. Despite extreme efforts, he had not succeeded in fulfilling his sense of responsibility. The regression therapy, and his subsequent insight into the origin of his drives, have helped Bill realize that he has to find a new perspective on life. The way in which he approaches relationships is now changing. Bill is finally learning to allow others to be themselves. He is no longer striving to win a game that cannot be won.

A Ph.D. in The Womb

My clients have included many successful people, among them businessmen and women, doctors, lawyers, writers, teachers, and other therapists. But their success has often come at some cost. In regression sessions, many of them were startled to remember feeling driven to excel even in the womb. And those memories of striving included the fervent wish to gain recognition from others for their work. As children, these individuals strove to distinguish themselves in school; as they grew older they made great efforts to achieve distinction in their chosen careers.

This pattern was true for Karen, a personable and attractive Canadian woman in her late twenties, already the head of a private social agency. Here are some excerpts from the information that Karen gave during her regression:

> *I am longing to go back to the spirit and the lightness. Here [in the womb] I am tied down and restricted. I feel it a lot! I feel sadness for being constrained in a physical form. I feel a tremendous impatience and am very tense. I am filled with energy and I need to get going!*

We took at look at Karen's parents as the pregnancy was progressing. She reported:

> *My father feels that his wife's pregnancy has nothing to do with him, he's not really a part of it. It's "just a pregnancy." He is concerned that nothing go wrong, but he doesn't express his concern and he stays separate from my mother.*

Karen's mother, meanwhile, was having a difficult time of it.

> *My mother is worried and is feeling overwhelmed. She is fearful and tense, and I pick up her tension very strongly. The tension is always there as an undercurrent. She is worried about the pregnancy and the delivery, she has to do it all alone. She is angry at him for his lack of support.*

As Karen's mother became angrier at her husband for not supporting her, he withdrew from her all the more, strongly affected by her anger. By the seventh month, the parents were hardly speaking to one another.

Whose side did Karen take? Her sympathies became apparent before too long:

> *I want to leave and get out. I am shielding myself from my mother, withdrawing into myself. When I withdraw, I get calmer. It is as though I have already separated from her and am aware of her from a distance.*

Karen's reaction against her mother puzzled me. I had expected her to align with her mother, who at so vulnerable a time received no support from her husband. But Karen's predisposition led her to align with her father, instead. Approaching the end of the pregnancy, Karen's mother became calmer, accustomed, perhaps, to her husband's emotional distance. But Karen's response to her mother did not change:

> *I feel separate and more resigned. I have a strong feeling of sadness and isolation. I am more closed to my mother than to my father. I am angry at her! My father is opening up to me, feeling some joy about the child-to-be. I can feel it!*

But immediately before the birth, the pressure on Karen in creased:

> *My mother wants a boy—or rather, she wants to give a boy to my father. She senses that I am a girl, and she is terribly disappointed. I feel that she does not want me.*
>
> *I am not special, I feel rejected. I will show her! I will be special. I will have power like a man, but I will not give up being female. I will gain power by being a woman. I will be visible and powerful the way males are, but by expressing love as a female.*

So Karen's urge for success sprang from her disappointment and anger over not feeling "special." Karen made a significant decision, a decision that strongly influenced the direction of her life, and her choice of career. Even early in her life she knew she would become a social worker. It met her needs. It gave her the opportunity to gain power in the world and yet to express her feminine identity through love and caring for others.

The feeling of "needing to get going" and moving ahead is familiar to Karen. It is, even now, a motivating force enabling her to achieve success and recognition. At a party celebrating the completion of her P.h.D. degree, Karen was asked to say a few words, and she described the years of exertion required to earn her degree. At one moment she caught my eye and smiled as we shared a secret. Of everyone present, only we two knew that her effort had begun before she was born.

8

Male and Female

Angie: "I will show him that he can be proud , even though I am a girl."

Do unborn infants always know if they are male or female? And if so, do they always accept their gender? What happens when they don't? How does the unborn infant react when he knows one or both parents prefer the other gender? Angie was caught in her parents' bias for a son. Her story provides some answers, and an ending that certainly surprised me.

They Wanted a Boy but Got a Baby

In the first months of the pregnancy, everything seemed to go well. In her regression, Angie reported:

> *My mother is rubbing her tummy and feels the growth within her. She is excited about the pregnancy. My father is also excited. He's worried about financial responsibilities but he definitely does want the baby.*

As the pregnancy progressed, her mother's excitement grew. Angie said:

> *She is getting a glow about her, as though my energy has been added to hers and is making her happy. But she wants a boy to*

please Dad. Their first child is a girl. Dad now wants a son to pass on the family name. They are both saying it doesn't matter, but I can tell that they really want a boy. I know there is a difference between "boy" and "girl," but it doesn't mean much to me.

By the fourth month, Angie's awareness of being female became heightened, along with her discomfort. She said:

Up until now I was just me. Now I know I am not a boy. Oh oh, I will throw a wrench into things! I am getting the idea that I will not be what they want. They say they will be happy either way, but I know that my dad prefers to have a boy. I want to please them so they aren't disappointed. What can I do?

Angie felt her parents' love and excitement, but her overriding concern was whether she would be acceptable as a female. She demanded to know:

Why does it have to be a boy? What's wrong with me? It hurts me and I get angry, mostly at Dad. I am more concerned to please my father than my mother.

Angie was forced to come to terms with the dilemma of being a girl when her father wanted a boy. She described her decision:

I will show him that he can be proud even though I am a girl. I will excel and be extraordinary. I will carry on the family tradition and name!

Based on similar prenatal histories, I might have expected Angie to emotionally separate herself from her father, for protection. But instead she took a head-on approach. She said:

I am assertive, directing lots of energy toward my father. I will make it up to him. "Dad, I'll make it worth it for you by giving you a lot of love. I'll show you!"

However, Angie's confidence was shaken. At the eighth month, she said:

I don't know how they will respond. I feel I have a lot to give them but I am not sure it will be enough. I am nervous about the birth. How will they take it when they find out I'm a girl?

Angie's fear had a negative effect upon the birth. At the time of birth, she reported:

I am making the birth hard because I am struggling! I struggle to move and then I stop. I get afraid to go on, but then I do. Now my head is out, but I'm stuck! My mom is in pain.

I decide to just go and do it! But my shoulders are holding me back. They can't get through. The opening is not big enough! I'm scared....There! I'm out! I'm out! Relief! But it's cold out here and much too bright.

I didn't want to come out. I was hiding in the womb to protect my identity as a girl. That's what made it so hard for my mom.

The doctor is holding me upside down—I don't like that. I start yelling, but it doesn't bother them—it makes them happy! The doctor cuts the cord. Someone rubs my skin and wraps me in something. I feel warm. My mom doesn't see me; she's tired. It was a hard and painful birth.

Angie was in for a surprise. Her father's reaction to his new baby girl was far from what she had expected:

My dad is happy! It blows my mind! I'm not a boy, but he still seems to be proud and happy. He's glowing! He shows no disappointment at all. He can't wait to show me to my mom.

Now I'm being taken to my mom. She is very tired, but she smiles when she sees me. She loves me too! There are no thoughts of boys now. I'm amazed and confused. I am a real blessing for them. There's a lot of love here for me. They are so happy to have a healthy baby.

A Female Proves Her Worth

The living presence of a newborn child sometimes transcends the parents' gender preference. Angie so delighted her father that his ideal of having a son became inconsequential to him. Here was his child, a newborn baby to love and care for! But after months of fear while in the womb, Angie's apprehension had become so deeply embedded that she could not completely trust her parents' joy in having a baby girl. So in spite of their acceptance of her, Angie never did let go of her earlier decision to make amends for being a girl. She repeated that decision immediately after birth: "I still feel the need to make amends. I choose to prove myself."

Through her childhood and into adulthood, Angie followed her prenatal vow to direct energy and love towards her father. Of his three daughters, she became his favorite. She sought constantly to excel. Like her father, she is a dedicated athlete who works out daily. She has entered into the same profession as her father. He is a lawyer, she a legal assistant. She even married a lawyer! Managing her husband's office, she assists her husband as she did her father. Angie extends her rigorous expectations for herself to her husband's employees as well.

Oh yes—true to her prenatal vow to carry on the family name, she has retained her own family name even after marriage!

Rejecting a Newborn of the "Wrong" Gender

It may come as a surprise to some readers to learn that there really are parents whose gender biases are strong enough to cause them to reject the newborn who doesn't measure up. Why would they reject their own child, rather than greet the child with love and a welcome?

Ideas about gender and sexuality have a lot of charge in our society. Distrust of the opposite gender is not uncommon. Sometimes we may feel undesirable or unequal to other men or women. Some men are competitive with other men; some women with other women. That competitiveness may even extend to rejecting a child who is of the same gender as oneself. A mother may be jealous of her husband's attention to their daughter, or a father of his son's closeness with his wife. In such cases, the parent may have an underlying fear that the marriage partner will prefer the child, and would rather spend time with the child than with the partner. This sense of competition sometimes remains dormant until puberty, erupting when the child's sexual development becomes pronounced.

Parental sensitivities in these areas can determine preferences for a son or a daughter. It is because we are struggling with emotional reactions that are difficult for us, because we are reacting to conditions that may come from our own earliest experiences, that we relate to our children in biased ways. Because of our gender biases, we withhold love from our unborn children without being aware that we are doing so. Unfortunately, this can deeply affect our unborn infants, who take very personally and very seriously the attitudes and emotions that guide our adult lives. Prenatal regression work makes very clear the fact that the children are both the physical and the psychological offspring of their parents.

Protect All Women

We've seen that an unborn infant may have a real need to please his mother and/or father. But when this doesn't work, he will try to find a strategy that will make him more acceptable to them. In pursuing his strategy, the infant may form an adaptation to life that has far-reaching consequences. The ideas and attitudes taken at that time may point the direction of life to follow, as it did in the following case.

John is thirty-eight years old and very attractive to women. His focus has always been toward females and he has few, if any, male friends. John has the square-jawed, rugged good looks of a "Marlboro Man," yet he appears sensitive and nurturing. He owns a beautiful sailboat which enhances his romantic image. His masculine manner joined with sensitivity have proven very attractive to women. Yet his relationships with them have usually been disasters for those women who have become emotionally involved.

Interestingly, John's intent through all of these relationships has not been to seduce or use women—it has been to take care of them! He began his regression by describing his mother:

> *She has been hanging out with a rough crowd. It looks like she enjoys living dangerously—drugs, gambling, and such. Her boyfriend is one of the men in this rough crew.*

"How does she happen to be with these people?" I asked.

> *She is from Argentina and she wants to become an American citizen. She hopes to meet someone who will marry her, and she will do whatever is needed to make that happen.*

John then described his father:

> *He acts like a tough guy, but he really has a good heart. That's the man who is my natural father. She has been trying to get him to marry her. Hoping he will marry her, she becomes pregnant. She is using him to become a citizen and he is using her for sex.*

But her plan to entrap a husband by becoming pregnant failed. In describing the experiences of the second month, John said:

> *Everything is unsettled and upsetting! She has told him that she is pregnant, but he puts her off. She wants him to marry her but she isn't sure he will. There is chaos all around! I am thinking "Oh, brother, what did I get myself into?"*

Looking at the situation a month later, John said:

Things are not much better. She is beginning to think he will not marry her. She's really angry at him. It's not working out as she had expected it to. He seems irresponsible.

John was able to clearly see his mother's manipulation, but he still felt sympathetic toward her. Feeling pressured by the situation, John made an important decision. He decided to take on responsibility for his mother's well-being. During the third month, he said:

I am going to be born to be a friend to her, to this person who doesn't have a friend in the world. I'll be her pal, a nice kid. It will be a good thing for her to have me!

John's mother was uninterested in the child in her womb; she didn't send nurturing thoughts his way. But John seemed to accept that. He said:

There's not much attention to me. She doesn't focus on me and I don't focus very much on myself. I am preoccupied with my mother. I don't feel badly that I am not getting love, only that she is not getting any.

The sixth and seventh months found John's mother in a dark mood.

My father was away but he has come back. She's trying to make him feel awful by laying a heavy guilt trip on him. She is blaming him, calling him a bastard—and she believes it herself. She takes on the role of being the victim. She doesn't like men but she needs their support.

John had a totally different view of his father. He said:

He has been getting more interested in me. He is smiling, good-willed. He now feels a part of all of this. He hopes for a son. I know he is warm and he cares about my welfare.

John's mother was becoming more resentful toward all men, damning them while scarcely acknowledging her own manipulation of them. John, who was sensitive and perceptive even in the womb, understood this but he still felt sympathetic and responsible for her.

> *I know she is blaming him—but that doesn't change my wanting to help this lady out. I make it okay that I don't get appreciation from her. I am all the more resolute to help her.*

By the eighth month, John's father had had all he could take of the blame being laid on him, and he left. So it was just John and his mother.

> *I need love, but I am not letting her know that. She is not sure she can handle a baby, so I say to her, "It's going to be okay. I'll be your pal. I won't be a troublesome kid."*

The labor and birth were difficult. John's mother kept resisting—all she could think of, even at that crucial time, was to blame the man who had gotten her pregnant. I asked John what was happening after the birth.

> *She provides for me, but emotionally she doesn't take care of me because I am a male. She is really distrustful of men and of life. Although I know she is not viewing things objectively, I feel myself developing a distrustful attitude like hers.*

Although he had pretended otherwise, John's relationship with his mother had caused him sadness and hurt. His mother had not expressed affection toward him, and it really was difficult for the defenseless infant to face his mother's negligence. However, he played the role of the little man, helping and acting as though he was not needy or weak. He buried his hurt.

Now, John the adult has a different view of his infancy:

> *She should have felt joyous, but I wasn't important! She blocked her feelings for me because of her anger at my father. I felt I didn't matter. I decided to be a strong, good baby to cheer her up, she was often so depressed.*

John is now thirty-eight years old. Yet his relationships with women are still patterned after his early experiences in the womb. He tries to excessively protect women and take responsibility for them, as he had done with his mother. Without giving thought to it, he assumes that women are not able to guide their own lives, and he chooses women who are needy. He is usually sure that he knows what is "right" for the woman.

His focus has always been toward females, as it had been toward his mother. His flirtatious manner is designed to charm women, and he has perfected his ability to be a charmer. He still plays that role even though he has been married for several years. He has not had any close male friends, a condition reminiscent of his never having had a relationship with his own father.

One side of John is very solicitous of women. But the hurt side has caused him to keep an emotional distance from them. He appears quite sensitive and nurturing, so that women open up to him. They fail to realize that he is not bonding to them. Several times he has ended long-term relationships by abruptly separating from his partners.

A strong carryover from John's prenatal experience showed itself in his reaction to having a child. Several years after their marriage, his wife became pregnant. John adamantly demanded that she have an abortion or he would leave her. He was prompted by an underlying reaction born of his own difficult prenatal experience. Much as his wife wanted to have a child, John would not yield, nor was he at all sensitive to her maternal response to the pregnancy. John's threat that he would leave her prevailed and she ended the pregnancy by having an abortion.

John has a magnetic charm and seems unusually self-sufficient as a person. There is no obvious reason for him to change. Yet the effect of the prenatal experience lives on in him. Deep within himself he feels a deprivation—he lacks the loving feeling of a nurtured infant. His underlying feeling of deprivation feeds his sardonic humor.

John began to change as a result of his regression experiences. In his therapy, he began the process of supporting and nurturing his unborn infant.

Becoming Homosexual

Brian faced a dilemma during his prenatal period. He could not side with either of his parents in their struggle with each other. He had no one to go to for love, support, and nurturing. In his work with me, Brian discovered that his preference for his own sex grew out of the constraint he felt with his parents.

At the start of the gestation period, Brian felt "nervous and edgy." His mother was angry that she was pregnant. She felt burdened. Brian, her second child, would add to her already oppressive load.

He, like John, responded to his mother by feeling sympathetic to her. He said:

> She doesn't want to be pregnant! I want to comfort her but it would not make any difference. She is angry and tired. It leaves me disconnected from her, with a feeling of isolation.

"What about your father?" I asked. Brian described his father as dominant, demanding, and aggressive. His father was traditional in his values and assertive in his role as head of the family. He worked hard to support the family, and demanded that his wife do her part in the home. But his appearance of strength was an illusion. He was emotionally dependent on his wife.

Brian's mother resented her husband's attitude and resisted him. She withheld from him the nurturing he so much needed. Although he scarcely recognized his need for affection, and lived by the ideal of being the strong and self-sufficient male, he was quite affected by her.

At the beginning of the gestation, Brian felt sympathetic to his mother. He felt guilty for being a burden to her. As for his father, Brian condemned him for being harsh and overbearing. Observing the events of the third month, Brian said, "Things are the same—he, with his male attitude, is demanding; she is trying to manage and is worn out. There is always high anxiety here."

By the sixth month, however, Brian's attitude toward his mother began to change. He spoke of his parents' interaction:

My mother doesn't respond—he has to control her! He is trying to maintain his male image of being in charge, especially in the eyes of his own parents. He needs affection, but isn't getting any.

Brian was now becoming reactive to his mother's hidden power. As the birth approached, Brian became even more affected, especially as his mother's attitude toward males became clearer to him. He said, "My mother wants another girl. She loves my sister, my sister is her only support." Brian felt guilty, knowing that he would not be the female his mother wanted. "I am unacceptable to her."

How was Brian to identify himself as a male? He recognized that "I don't want to be the boy my father wants me to be. I don't like my father." Brian had already rejected his father as harsh and demanding during the early months of the pregnancy. But, he could not align with his mother either, since she was unwilling to accept males.

In an attempt to appease his mother, Brian failed to identify himself as a male like his father. The truth that Brian absorbed during the prenatal period was that women are threatening because they are more powerful than men. He feared his mother and withdrew emotionally from all women. It was the only way he knew to maintain himself. During his regression, Brian had an insight:

Actually, I am angry at my father because he couldn't control my mother. She is angry at all men. I feel my identity is threatened by my mother and by all women!

Brian did not find an effective way of dealing with the situation: "With my father, I never expressed my love. With my mother, I never expressed my anger." Brian feared to express his male force with women, to express his male identity. The unresolved emotions were turned inward. As a result he developed a fundamental evasiveness in his personality. In his homosexual orientation he found a protective shield that kept him emotionally safe.

There are many factors that contribute to sexual preference and the compassion, love, and hate that we feel for members of our own sex or the opposite one. However, in regression therapy we see, time and time again, that the roots of these very basic feelings begin with some of our earliest experiences.

When there are conflicts that limit our ability to enjoy the choices we have made in our adulthood, we can often resolve them by going back in time to retrace the most fundamental of our relationships—those we had with our own parents before we even emerged from the womb.

_9_

Birth

Jane: "I feel tremendous panic.
I am caught in the birth canal and can't get out."

Arthur Janov writes, "For many of us, birth is the closest we will come to death for the rest of our lives until we are truly at death's door." Jane's emotional birth experience, in which she was convinced she was dying, led to a misunderstanding that colored her entire life.

A Birth that Seemed like a Death

Jane described what had started out as a normal birth:

J: *I feel pressure, like waves. I'm being pushed real hard, and I'm in the middle of all this confusion.*

M: Okay, let's move you forward a bit. What's happening now?

J: *The nurse is near my mother. The nurse says something to her. She's tying my mother's legs together with something. Some kind of strap.*

M: Why does she tie your mother's legs together?

J: *The doctor is not here....He was told that he would not be needed until later. The nurse is panicked—the birth is coming too soon!*

M: Breathe deeply now. That's it. And how are you doing?

J: *I'm feeling an incredible pressure, but I'm stuck here. The pressure is bearing down on me. I feel like I'm being crushed, but I'm not moving forward.*

  I feel tremendous panic. I am caught in the birth canal and can't get out! The feeling of being closed in is horrible!! My head is aching!

  A rush of anger comes from my mother. [Pause.] I'm getting angry! How could she do this to me? I feel anger and panic all mixed together. Am I going to die? Maybe she doesn't want me. [Jane begins crying intensely here.]

M: Can you go on? What happens next?

J: *Now it's changing...it's better, easing up... a different kind of pressure. The doctor is here. I'm moving now. I'm not going to die! At last, I am born!*

  After I get born, I feel a great outpouring of love from my mother, but it confuses me—she was angry at me and didn't want me. How can I trust her? I want her love, but I also want to punish her. I'm angry about what happened.

The effects of the harsh birth experience were long lasting. Jane recognized that the claustrophobia she had experienced throughout her life, the sudden fear she felt whenever she found herself in a small enclosure, was a direct consequence of her experience while in the birth canal. She was repeatedly playing out the terror of being confined in the birth canal, and her fear of dying there. She was also hypersensitive to being slighted or disliked by others. If her own mother didn't want her, and was even trying to harm her, which was her assumption during the traumatic birth, why would anyone else care for her?

Jane's regression had been an intense, emotional one. When we reviewed her prenatal experience again, the reliving was easier for her. She had released some of her emotion during the earlier recall. This time, she was able to experience her birth more objectively.

M: Let's have you move ahead to the time when your mother's legs were strapped together by the nurse.

J: *The nurse had told the doctor that he wasn't needed until later, so she became frantic when the birth started going fast. So she ties my mother's legs together. My mother is panicking. She doesn't know what to do, and she is very distressed. My mother is furious.*

M: Breathe deeply, feel her anger, feel who the anger is directed toward.

J: *She's angry at the nurse! My mother really fears harm toward me. I assumed that her anger at the nurse was anger toward me. That was a serious mistake.*

Jane began to release the effects of the birth experience that had too long plagued her. As she reconnected with her mother's deep love for her, Jane felt a sense of completion. She said "I am connecting with her basic, unqualified love for me. I know I am wanted." After a while, she was able to release the fear and anger that had accumulated around her traumatic birth.

The Moment of Truth

For the infant, birth is the "moment of truth." The infant in the womb can no longer remain hidden, but must make a visible entrance into the outer world. For some infants, excited to greet the experiences of life, birth is the awaited moment, the opportunity which they have impatiently anticipated. Leaving the restriction of the womb, they experience birth as the entrance into a world in which they will be able to effectively express themselves, acting out their desires and aspirations. They face adventure in the spirit of those who came to the New World, a world filled with limitless possibilities.

But others have difficulty giving up the low visibility of the previous nine months. Hidden in the womb, they have not previously had to directly confront a threatening world in which they feel at risk. For these prenatal infants, birth is attended with trepidation, fear, or even dread. And then there are prenatal infants who expect that birth will relieve them of their distress. They anticipate that the change of setting and a more independent identity will release them from the pressures they have been experiencing. This is sometimes the case, but not always.

Birth is not a separate, isolated experience, nor is it simply a biological one. It is the culmination of nine months of intense experience for all involved: for the infant, mother, father, and the other family members. The birth experience itself will ordinarily be very much influenced by the conditions that existed during the gestation period. The emotional conditions and patterns of relationship established in the prenatal period often significantly affect the physical process of birth, even so far as to affect the ease or difficulty of the delivery itself.

A Caesarean Birth

In Dale's case, his father had not wanted a child, but his mother did, and she contrived to get pregnant against his wishes. They did not discuss separating, but there was tension between them all during the pregnancy. Prior to the birth, faced with the impending reality of a child, Dale's mother became more fearful and concerned, for she knew that she had countered her husband by getting pregnant. All of her energy was going into her anxiety, and she failed to nurture her child in the womb. Dale felt the change: "I feel rejected, and I react. I turn the wrong way, with my feet first."

The doctor's examination immediately before Dale's birth revealed the sudden change to a breech position, so the decision was made to deliver the baby by Caesarian section.

Another client, Hilda, obviously a feisty personality, had a similar experience. Angry and resentful because of her mother's ambivalence about having another child, Hilda turned around in the womb, saying "If she wants me, then let her come and get me!" And a Caesarean section was the only way to get her!

A Premature Birth

A premature birth sometimes indicates a prenatal infant in distress. The pressure may be so intolerable that the infant feels compelled to escape from the womb. Pam certainly felt strong emotions during her gestation. At first she reported:

> *I feel a sense of wonderment and joy from my mother. I don't feel much from my father, he seems bewildered.*

After a few weeks had passed:

> *My mother is preoccupied with her relationship to my father. She wants more from him; he is rather disconnected from her.*

And then by the sixth month:

> *My mother is fearful and desperate. She doesn't feel prepared to have me. She is not receiving any support from my father and she does not know what to do.*

Meanwhile, Pam had drawn closer to her mother. She said:

> *I am sympathetic to my mother. When she gets upset, I try to stay strong and ward it off. My father fades in and out. I feel disassociated from him. I don't know if he is really there!*

By the seventh month, it was all becoming too much. Pam said:

> *I am not feeling good. I wish this were all a dream. I am feeling the frustrations of my parents and loving them at the same time. I feel their emotions coming into me and I don't understand them. Things are not as they should be! I am wondering if this is all my responsibility. I wonder if I've chosen the right parents or if they made the right choice in picking me. I feel so sad. Time goes by and there is no relief!*

Reaching her limit in the eighth month, Pam exclaimed:

*I need to get out! They are not focusing on my development.
They're so caught up in themselves that I'm not getting the nurturing I need. I'm giving up on them ever becoming aware of me.*

*I make a decision. I would rather leave and start over! I love
them both, but I'm taking the next step and saying "This is it!" I
don't know where I will go or what will happen. But the emotional
pain is so extreme that I must get out. I want to get away at all
costs!*

However it came about, Pam was born prematurely during
the eighth month. She could not recall going through the birth
process. The next thing she remembered was being enclosed in an
incubator. She said:

*I'm breathing such a sigh of relief! I have a love feeling from the
nurses and others—it's wonderful! A healing place. I have no
sense of my mother or father, but I don't feel a lack. I enjoy the
quietness. It's so peaceful here I just want to stay.*

Hardly what one might have expected! Others have felt isolated and forgotten in the incubator, but Pam found it to be a sooth-
ing place. Fortunately, Pam was able to heal the distress she had
felt during the preceding months. Although her parents had not
resolved their differences by the time she arrived home, she was
not as sensitive to their relationship. She said:

*What is different is that I am no longer receiving information and
feelings through the umbilical cord. I now receive differently.
Before, my raw nerves were so sensitive.*

*My physical organs are not developed completely. They are still
being healed. That brings discomfort to me but I know I will be
healed in time. I'm often hungry because I can't eat a lot at one
time. I keep my parents awake with my hunger. I have a sense that
things will now be okay.*

The Power of the Prenatal Infant

A view of prenatal infants as helpless victims does not encompass the whole truth. Not all infants feel powerless. Rather than being merely passive and affected by uncongenial conditions in the womb or after birth, some prenatal infants take effective and powerful actions. These infants report that they were able to influence the conditions of their birth. Their ability to affect the onset and ease of the birth process is notable, and supports the belief that we human beings possess scarcely recognized resources within ourselves to influence the world around us.

A Convenient Birth

Regressed to the very beginning of the pregnancy, Patricia was exhilarated. She said, "I am feeling a lot of power in myself. I want to be here! I feel very high and adventurous." By the second month, her parents realized that she was on the way. Her mother was in turmoil. Patricia reported:

> *She is not sure what to do with me! She already has a child who is thirteen months old. After the child was born, she caught on to how limiting children can be. She doesn't want to spend her life changing diapers. She has a desire to express herself in business. She is a strong, stubborn woman.*

And then, during the third month:

> *I will do anything I can to be born. I am hiding, hoping she won't notice me. Part of me says Mom's right, that I should go away and not bother her life. But I make a decision. I'll be as stubborn as my mother. I decide to stay, but I feel guilty. I decide to be born anyway.*

In the seventh month:

I'm getting too big to hide! I'm trying to be quiet, so I don't move much. I feel guilty about being a burden, so I resolve to help her after I am born.

When the pregnancy came to term, Patricia's influence on the birth was remarkable.

I decide to make this birth as easy as possible. I arrange to get born at evening. I didn't even keep my mother up late or keep my father from work! It is a quick and easy birth. I am so pleased with myself. I hardly cry at all.

Patricia subconsciously remembered the decision she had made while in the womb, to help her mother later. She became a self-reliant child who dutifully assisted her mother with household chores. She honored her pledge.

I Leave at the Earliest Moment I Can

Gary also created a premature birth, deciding early on in the pregnancy that he would leave the womb as soon as he was able to survive on his own. In the regression, he immediately sensed his parents' discord:

My mother believes that it is not right to have a child. She and my father had agreed to have no more children.

She is very angry at him because he doesn't support her. When she tries to speak to him, he gets enraged, so she backs off. She is so confused—blaming my father, then feeling inadequate. She cares a lot but she wishes I wasn't there.

At times, her anger extended even to her unborn child. Gary said, "Sometimes she scares herself when she directs her anger at me. She is trapped on the outside by her husband, trapped on the inside by me." His mother's emotional vacillation was not easy for Gary:

I do not know what to expect. I know she loves me, but she is con-fused. Her love is blocked. I fear that she might hurt me! I am not secure in just being here—if I let go, I will die!

Trying to deal with the difficult circumstances, Gary said:

I consider making an early escape. Maybe something is wrong with me that this is all happening. I keep feeling that it's me. I take responsibility, trying to console her. I don't want to take nourishment—I believe it drains her. She doesn't have enough for herself!

Gary continued expressing concern for his mother:

I need her, but I don't want to deprive her. I want to get out to relieve her, but I can't get out yet because I'm not whole.

He was in a dilemma. But by the end of the seventh month, Gary knew that he had received all that he needed in order to live. He said:

I can make it on the outside now. My mother and I have sustained each other—now we must let go. It is time for me to leave. She will do better with me out.

The early birth was easy for both Gary and his mother. The premature baby was, indeed, very fragile. But Gary was able to survive. He had resolved his prenatal dilemma.

The period immediately following the birth is also critical. You might expect that an infant who was wanted and loved while in the womb and who has had a relatively easy birth, would not be especially vulnerable immediately after being born. But this is not necessarily the case. The sensitive newborn is characteristical-ly open and susceptible to outer influences. This is a crucial time, as reports in the next chapter indicate, and the comfort of a loving touch cannot be overemphasized.

10

Experiences After Birth

Sharon: "I'm already a person, I want them to know that."

Barbara joked that after nine difficult months in the womb, no matter what happened after birth, it would be a great relief. But during her regression an unexpected note of anxiety crept into her voice:

> *I'm a little afraid because I'm going to have to rely on other people. I'll be in the hands of the doctors and nurses. I hope they'll take good care of me!*

Her fear became even more pronounced as the birth approached. She couldn't disguise her reluctance to be born:

> *I just feel scared and insecure! As bad as it's been, I've been protected and I haven't had too much to worry about.*

The experiences following her birth confirmed Barbara's fears:

B: *I want to be close to my mom. Nobody's concerned about me, the doctors or anybody else! They're just handling me like a piece of meat! I don't feel any sense of security. I don't get it from my mother. I just feel very alone!*

M: What's happening with your mother?

B: *She's just too tired and doesn't care. I'm just another one to take care of, as far as she's concerned. [She sighs deeply.]*

[She starts sobbing.] The birth was extremely hard for me. I am put down somewhere, left all alone. Somewhere in the hospital, I guess. I'm all alone.

I'm scared! At least in the womb I had the security of being someplace. I didn't have anything physical to worry about. Now I have to trust these people to take care of me.

It would be great if someone would hold me, that would make a lot of difference. I just need someone to hold me and love me, to have physical closeness.

I thought it would be a relief to be born, but it's hard to be separated from the constant physical presence—I want to be with my mother again! I want to have that sense of protection and security.

Traumas with Enduring Consequences

Dr. Janov states, "If ever there was a key trauma with lifelong consequences it is the separation of the newborn from its mother right after birth. As if the long birth struggle had not been enough; as if the harsh delivery room conditions had not been enough—the infant is then actually taken away from the one person who has been its entire source of comfort, its entire world." We take a look at some "lifelong consequences" of abrupt separation from mother, and see how important decisions are made at that critical time.

"Nobody cares!" That was Susan's impression. She said of her earliest relationships:

The birth was difficult. My mother is out, drugged—she didn't want to feel it. My father is not here, he didn't want to come into the delivery room.

I am scared. I feel unwanted. My mom just wants to rest and my father isn't here. I have a burning hunger, but no one is doing anything about it. They put me away in the nursery. I want to be fed and touched and held, but no one cares!

I Learned to Not Ask

Sam was born by emergency Caesarean section.

My mother is struggling. She is not in good physical condition, and there are complications. Everyone seems worried. My mother cannot hold me any longer. The birth is sudden—a flash of light and I am out.

I want to nurse and be close to my mother, but everyone is concentrating on making sure she is okay. I am picked up by a nurse and taken away. I want someone to hold me and keep me warm, but no one knows how I feel. I stop expecting help. I learned to not ask for what I wanted.

An Angry Response

Emily had a positive prenatal experience; she felt her parents' love for her. Looking forward to her birth with anticipation, she reported: "My mother and father are in harmony, yes. They do love each other. They are eager for me to be born."

The birth process went smoothly, but, in accordance with a standard hospital procedure, Emily was taken from her mother immediately following the birth. That lonely time was very difficult for her:

I am alone and sad! I am afraid no one will come. There is nothing I can do. I thought I would be close with my mother and father, but everyone is gone. I feel unprotected, isolated, and sad. I want someone to come and get me!

How did this helpless infant react to such isolation?

I'm getting mad—I'll do it by myself. I'll show them! I hate them! Maybe they forgot about me. I'm afraid—I don't know anyone else in the world.

I'm starting to think something's wrong with me. I am overwhelmed with sadness and grief, feeling very sorry for myself. How do you get someone to take care of you?

By the time the nurses arrived to bring Emily to her mother, the hurt had gone too deep. She said:

I am glad they are here, but I won't let them know I am glad. I can't let go of the sadness. The sadness seems more like the truth.

As an adult, Emily still carries that deep wound within herself. She said, "That is the same sadness I often have now, the sadness of being alone, of not being connected to others." Her emotional predisposition as an adult was established in those crucial moments after her birth.

This feeling was also involved in Emily's strong desire, at the age of twenty-four, to have a child. She said, "I want to love a baby. I want to give the love I didn't get. If I can't have a child, I will feel all alone."

Emily wants to heal her early isolation by having a child, by reexperiencing, in the reverse role of mother, her own infant beginnings. As a therapist, I would be concerned for the child she would bear. That child might well carry the burden of supporting a mother whose emotional core is still that of the needy and isolated newborn infant.

Happy Births

Fear, isolation, and sadness are not everyone's experience at birth. I always gladly welcome the stories of happy births, like those of Sharon, who felt wanted and contented after her birth. Describing the birth experience, she said, "I am being born! I come out crying, but it is a cry of life. I am happy to be who I am. I like being a female. I am already a person—I want them to know that! I know I won't be a weakling."

Sharon said that the doctor who was present at her birth liked her. She said, "I stop crying and I am pleasant, showing him that I am glad to be here." She continued:

> *I like the attention here. It makes me feel comfortable. My mother is making me comfortable, too. She feeds me—I enjoy that. She likes nursing, too! She is glad to have me here. I go to sleep, feeling contented and safe. My mother sleeps, too. I feel good and safe by her, in harmony.*

Within a few hours, Sharon's father came to visit. She reported:

> *He picks me up. He thinks I'm great! He is pleased and proud. I feel good to be welcomed. He leans over, kisses my mother, and congratulates her on having me! She says she will name me Sharon. I feel identified.*

Sharon described the period following her birth:

> *I am bringing happiness to them! My needs are met and I am being taken care of with joy. She will be a good mother to me.*

Many mothers intuitively recognize that their feelings of love and caring are significant sources of comfort for their unborn and newly-born infants. However, our society as a whole is only beginning to speculate that the thoughts and feelings of parents are actually communicated to the baby. We look forward to a time when our society acknowledges the unborn child's level of awareness. May the day soon arrive when each human being experiences a warm welcome into the world!

_11_

Miscarriage and Stillbirth

Becky: "I took all the life out, and I left."

Unready Parents

Mary's prenatal regression had an unexpected twist right from the beginning, when she reported, "Something's wrong. I don't understand! I'm a male!" It made no sense, and Mary didn't know what to make of it.

We went forward to the first month of the pregnancy and began to search for an explanation. I asked Mary, "Are you in the womb now?"

I am in the vicinity, but I hold back from entering my body. I want to stay detached. I am reluctant to come in. It seems like I am taking on a lot. I'm nervous, and it feels like a big risk.

But Mary involuntarily lost her detachment at the end of the first month:

My mother has found out she is pregnant. When she realizes this, I can no longer remain outside. A connection opens, and I am immediately pulled into her body. It's as though her awareness sucks me into her body. I lose my separateness. I am a part of my mother now, without a sense of myself. It's as if you could see right through me.

As the gestation continued, Mary showed real insight into her parents' relationship. She observed:

My mother is not feeling well. One of the reasons she is sick is because she dislikes her body and its physical functions. She is always thinking badly about herself. She tries to ward off her husband's affection, but, at the same time, she encourages his dependence on her because it gives her control. She despises him for what she believes is his weakness, and she fears that he will be inadequate as a father.

His wife's self-absorption in the pregnancy was difficult for her husband. Mary sensed his discomfort intensely and said of him:

He is feeling excluded. He is needy and dependent on my mother. He feels left out because she focuses on the pregnancy. It's almost like there is one adult—my mother—and two children—my father and me. He is competing with me for my mother's attention.

As the pregnancy continued, Mary said, "My father is getting more angry at being shut out. He is hardening into anger." The young husband did not dare to directly express the anger he felt at his wife. He blamed the unborn infant instead. Reliving that experience, Mary felt herself reeling from the impact of his anger, spinning uncontrollably. His wife also sensed his anger. Mary said, "My mother is frightened. She thinks his anger is directed at her." Her mother's strategy for dealing with that anger added to Mary's confusion:

Now my mother is beginning to open up to me, but it seems wrong somehow. Oh, now I see! She begins to open to me to create an alliance with me against my father. She is going to use me to maintain control over my father. She relates to me only in terms of her relationship to her husband.

The Cause of Death

The unborn male child in the womb received virtually no nurturing energy or support. His father was angry and in rivalry with him, and his frightened mother was manipulative. In the seventh month, Mary recognized that:

> *My father sees me as a rival. I can't function without getting my mother's love and acceptance, but that won't happen—my mother doesn't like or trust males. I, myself, am confused about being a male. It's much easier and more comfortable for me to be a female.*

Mary described how difficult it had become for her:

> *I am nervous in my stomach, feeling the strain. It's all mixed up, a charade. I am in limbo; there is no place for me here. They direct no energy toward me. I don't know what to do! It's getting to be more than I can live with.*

The strain was beginning to have an extreme effect, and Mary was hitting her limits. In a voice which reflected her low energy level and depletion, Mary said, weakly:

> *I feel strong pressure to my stomach and head. I am losing life, and I have no connection to sustain me. It's too much for me. I feel a hopelessness, a pending doom. I am losing all my energy.*

In the ninth month, in a voice filled with emotion, she said:

> *It's as though I have no choice. Although my body is healthy, I withdraw, feeling sadness, but also deep relief. I leave the body during the middle of the ninth month. I stay around in the vicinity.*

Absence of a Heartbeat

Mary stayed near her parents in her non-physical soul body. Within two days of her withdrawal, Mary's mother became consciously aware of the change. She felt no movement. Alarmed, she

went to the doctor, who could not find a heartbeat and who confirmed a probable stillbirth. Mary said:

> *When they found out the child was no longer alive, that was the
> first time they stopped being so wrapped up in themselves and
> recognized that their child had been a living, separate person.*

The young parents grieved over their loss. Mary said, "They
fear that they are inadequate. But underneath, each blames the
other for the child's death." However, their mutual grief furthered
their maturity and personal connection.

What were Mary's feelings as she reexamined that death? Self-
blame and regret. She described it this way:

> *I feel guilty for causing them so much unhappiness. If I had had
> more individuality, I could have been born. I identified with
> them—but not with myself. I just didn't have the support I needed
> to make it. There was nothing to pull me through.*

The Second Try

Mary reported that she "came back in" (meaning into a physical form) about six months later. Her mother was once again pregnant; the same soul that had once entered her womb had now
reentered it. This time, however, that same soul had a female body.

Though the parents had learned from their experience, unresolved emotions still abounded. Mary said:

> *My mother very much fears losing this child, as she lost the other.
> She grieves and feels guilty for the stillbirth, she fears that she will
> fail as a wife if she can't birth a live child. My father feels guilty,
> too. He somehow connects his feelings of inadequacy with the loss
> of the child. And I feel an overriding sense of guilt for causing my
> mother such grief.*

The sadness and grief made the atmosphere in the womb
onerous for the prenatal infant. Mary felt guilty and responsible

for her parents' grief—hadn't she deprived them of their first child? This made the situation almost unbearable for her. As the last trimester approached, Mary's mother was intensely frightened. What if she gave birth to another stillborn child? Mary, surrounded by her mother's panic, had to do something; but this time she was able to make a different choice than before.

> *I don't want to be in here anymore! It's too oppressive to live in this darkness and fear. I'm always feeling my mother's nervousness. She never talks about it to anyone, but she is always carrying her guilt and inadequacy. I make a decision to get born, and I do so.*

Mary was born at the beginning of the seventh month. Shortly after the birth, the fragile infant was placed in an incubator. Mary remarked: "It feels so good to finally be separate from her. Such a relief. "

Mary's mother never fully recovered from the loss of her first child. Neither did Mary. To make up for the pain she had caused her mother, during her childhood Mary acted as though she were responsible for her mother's emotional well-being. It was easy for her father to get her to behave, for any time his wife was upset, he had only to say, "Look what you've done to your mother!"

Opening to the memories of these early experiences was the first step that enabled Mary to resolve her lingering sadness and guilt at not being born the first time. She was now able to move into a clearer personal relationship with her parents, claiming the sense of personal identity that had been left unexpressed during those experiences more than thirty years before.

Tangible Emotions

Strong emotions coming from the mother, and sometimes from the father, may be felt by the infant in the womb as tangible sensations. Sometimes these sensations become overwhelming, and critical decisions are made as a result of the pressure. My client, Becky, reported in the sixth month of her gestation:

> *My head hurts. I feel drained because of all the emotion. It's getting heavier and heavier, like weights are being piled on me. I feel my parents' turmoil. I'm being battered by energy. It's making me so heavy.*

Becky did not know how to deal with her parents' distress over the pregnancy. She felt too fragile and was unable to accommodate the intense emotional atmosphere of the womb. Late in the sixth month, she exclaimed:

> *I feel like I'm being pushed, like I'm being smashed. All the air is coming out of me. I'm not going to be able to continue. The life is out of me. I got too heavy, so I took all the life out and I left.*

The result was a miscarriage during the sixth month. Near the end of her regression, Becky expressed a brief afterthought—she commented, ruefully, "I inhabited that body, a boy's body. I wanted to be born...so very much...but I died."

Tracing the Causes

As we have seen, some prenatal regressions bring to view a previous gestation which did not result in a live birth. Obviously, for these individuals to report this, a later gestation was successful for each of them. The occurrence of a stillbirth or a miscarriage brings deep unhappiness to most parents. They frequently struggle with grief after such an experience, wondering, "Why wasn't our child born alive?" The loss and sorrow strike deeply, and are often difficult to resolve.

No one reason or explanation can account for all uncompleted pregnancies. Each individual situation develops from a unique physical and/or emotional interaction between the mother, father, and the unborn infant. Physical malformations of the fetus cause some miscarriages. Emotional influences also cause miscarriages and stillbirths. How well are unborn infants able to weather the emotional storms that surround them? How able are they to confront the parental stress that results from poor marital relationships or family crises during the pregnancy, or such external conditions as poverty? As we have seen, in some cases, the answer is "Not well at all."

"I Deprived Them of a Sister"

My client Laurie was not a person whom one could ignore. A heavy-set, spirited woman, she sent out waves of intense emotion. Laurie often perceived others as criticizing her, even when that was not their intention. Any hint of criticism caused her to flare up in reaction.

To get to the root of her inordinate sensitivity to criticism, we investigated her prenatal experience. While speaking of her childhood, her mother's previous pregnancy flashed through her mind. She remarked, "Mother miscarried the baby that came before me. I've always gotten strange sensations when others speak of the baby being born dead."

In regression, Laurie continued to explore that earlier pregnancy. "It feels like there were two of us at the time of the previous miscarriage. I was a boy; the other was a girl." She said that her mother knew she was pregnant with twins, although the condition had not yet been medically confirmed.

Laurie explained her parents' situation at the time of that prior pregnancy. Their thoughts were not on raising a child, much less two children. Struggling to succeed financially, they were pouring tremendous energy and effort into their own fledgling business. They were ill-prepared to raise children with all the demands and adjustments that would be required.

Laurie revealed her own apprehension during that prior gestation:

> *I felt it wasn't right for me to be born as a boy. One time, my mother fell, and I used the opportunity to leave. I also caused my twin sister to leave. I didn't mean to take her with me! She left because of our connection. She followed my energy—I was the stronger of the two of us. I feel like I killed my other half!*

Laurie blamed herself for her sister's death and for depriving her parents of a daughter. That guilt carried over into the second pregnancy. Laurie was born eight years later, as a daughter to those same parents. By this time, and after considerable effort, her parents had begun to succeed in business. Laurie noted that her mother and father had become more secure within themselves, and were now better able to turn their attention and love to their unborn infant.

But Laurie, still carrying so much guilt, could not open herself up to receive her parents' love for her. She sobbed:

> *I don't know what to do! How can they love me when I killed my sister before? I am responsible for what happened! I can't accept the love being directed towards me.*

Laurie decided to make amends for the earlier miscarriage. She said, "I made the decision to be a loving, model child. I won't disappoint them! I'll be the best kid possible."

The birth did not take long. Laurie said, "I made the birth easy for my mother." But even after the birth, she could not get beyond feeling guilty, saying, "Everyone is delighted that I am here except for me."

Although much love was directed toward her by her parents, Laurie did not respond to that love, feeling unworthy of it. She said, "They expressed love toward me but I didn't believe it."

As an adult, Laurie had still been carrying the burden of the unrecognized and unresolved guilt from her first gestation. We saw that this was a prime cause for her acute sensitivity to criticism. Moreover, during the regression, Laurie saw that her twin sister had been physically weak and would have required a great deal of attention from unwilling parents.

In a later regression, Laurie saw the first gestation in a different light:

> *Had my sister been born, there would have been a lot of heartache and financial difficulties for my parents. It would have pushed my mother over the edge! She could handle the loss of a child more easily than having a constantly ill child to care for in those circumstances.*

Now a more positive picture emerged, in which the miscarriage was seen as appropriate for all concerned—for Laurie, her twin sister, and her parents. Once again a synchronicity was demonstrated, in which painful events were actually beneficial to the persons involved. Once Laurie recognized why those events had turned out as they did, she was better able to release the responsibility and guilt that had been so limiting to her, and to open herself to the love her parents and others have for her.

Life and Death Decisions

The accounts that we have sampled in this chapter are interesting because they tell us that some miscarriages and stillbirths are intentional—that the infant in the womb initiates them by deciding to separate from, and leave, the fetal body. They also give us an understanding of why some unborn infants are not willing or able to continue the gestation period. But they have a further importance, and that is to demonstrate that birth and death are only transitory stages in an enduring journey.

12

Connections and Disconnections

Carrie: "She is trying to love me—I can feel her heart—
but she doesn't want to get attached to me, knowing
that she will give me away after I am born."

Adoption

Carrie is the child of an unwed mother, a mother who became pregnant while still in her teens. Carrie's experience was a poignant and difficult one. Her story revealed the deep distress felt by a mother and infant who knew that they would not remain together after birth. During the fourth month of gestation, Carrie said:

> *My mother is in trauma. She has no husband and she doesn't know where to turn. I feel like I am suffocating. Things are pressing in. I wish we could get this over with! Or maybe that's my mother's feeling, I'm not sure. The outside influences feel chaotic; people are giving lots of advice to my mother and she must make decisions about this pregnancy.*

By then, Carrie's mother knew that she would have to give up her child for adoption and she handled the situation in the best way she knew:

> *There is a feeling of separate identity. We are not growing as one. She is trying to love me—I can feel her heart—but she doesn't*

133

want to get attached to me, knowing that she will give me away
after I am born. This is starting to be painful for both of us.

The intensity was building, and by the fifth month, Carrie
reported:

My mother is feeling self-pity, but there's nothing for me! There is
a lot of pain between us. We are close, but there is a barrier. I feel
anxiety all the time—just the same as I do now.

The emotional connection to the mother is the psychological
lifeline for the unborn infant, and when that connection is lacking,
anxiety and insecurity can result. Outside influences were also
entering the picture. Demonstrating the remarkable level of
awareness that is shown by some unborn infants, Carrie said:

I feel an attachment to someone else. It's my adoptive mother. Her
little boy is there also. She is waiting for me. She wants me, but all
the feelings about my mother crowd in for me, making things dif-
ficult.

In the seventh month, Carrie said:

I am more real to my mother now. We are more a part of each other.
She is still alone and afraid, feeling anxious. She has no contact
with my father. She wanted to have children in a family setting and
to feel loved. She feels much bitterness about the pregnancy.

Carrie was even able to sense the subliminal relationship
between her birth mother and her adoptive mother. She said,
"There is animosity between them. They feel jealousy and rivalry
toward one another."

Reflecting on her experience in the womb, Carrie said:

The whole thing has been mainly negative and unhappy for both
of us. I'm feeling anxiety all the time, now. This has been a strug-
gle and I'm worn out! The waves of energy I've been feeling are
waves of pain.

I feel guilty because my mother is unhappy, and I feel helpless because I can't do anything about it. My sadness is a pain in my stomach. I am angry, wondering "Why don't you love me?"

Carrie Decides to Be Born

Desperately wanting to escape the turmoil in the womb, Carrie created a premature birth during the seventh month. She briefly described how she did so: "In order to get out, I build intensity. It feels like I start the birth process." Carrie spent her first six weeks isolated in an incubator, and commented, "What complete calm! The calm after the turmoil feels so good."

Carrie was taken by her adoptive mother immediately afterwards. She was loved by her, and she called her "Mother" and loved her in return. But the emotional turmoil she had absorbed during the gestation never left.

She had suffered from chronic anxiety and insecurity for as long as she could remember. Through regression, we discovered that it was the same unresolved anxiety and insecurity she had felt in the womb. Understanding the origin of her anxiety was a first step in the process of Carrie's release of it. But there was another unfinished element.

Though she loves the mother that raised her, there is a part of Carrie that seeks the knowledge of her natal origin. She has a persistent desire to find her birth mother. The bond remains, although Carrie has been separated from her mother since birth, and all conscious memory of her has faded.

It is her desire to renew the love that joined them as mother and child. She feels the soul connection between them—and she wants to see and know her mother, again.

The Soul Enters Physical Reality

The common religious view in the West is that we are physical beings, who have souls that are non-physical and eternal. This view focuses on what happens to the soul after death. The usual belief is that the soul starts its activity at the beginning of one's current life, and continues on forever following death. Although it is not stated explicitly, it is implied that the soul incarnates one time only, and the experience of the soul for the rest of eternity is determined by the experiences during that incarnation, however brief.

The information obtained in these prenatal regressions reveals a different perspective. People report that they are conscious prior to conception. They report that they enter a fetal body, and then may leave it again, creating a miscarriage or stillbirth. These same beings, or souls, may reappear in a later pregnancy. Thus the regressions offer us a unique opportunity to more closely examine the remarkable connection between a human soul and its physical embodiment.

Soul Connections

The traditional view of family bonding is that children love their parents, and vice versa, because they are born to them. But in the light of our understanding from regressions, we know that children are born to particular parents because they have a strong soul connection with them.

We do not incarnate randomly. Parents and child come together in a way that is not casual or arbitrary. There is a "soul magnetism" that brings us together in close family interactions. The synchronicity of the universe works in a wondrous way to ensure that our interchanges with those we love provide growth and learning for all individuals involved—the mother, father, and all the children.

Our life connections with those whom we love are deeply affecting to us, and are critical in their effect upon our psychological and spiritual growth. Family ties are among the most profound inner, or soul, connections we may experience in a lifetime, sometimes supporting us by the depth of love and empathy expressed, and sometimes confronting us with most difficult conflicts.

Harmonious relationships may release a great deal of creative energy or they may challenge us to avoid stagnation; discordant relationships may limit our life energies or provide the means of liberating them. We grow considerably, sometimes even transforming ourselves, when we are able to resolve serious problems that have resulted from our relationships with others.

We normally assign to parents the role of teachers whose function it is to assist their children as they learn about the life process. Parents obviously do teach their children. But the reverse is also true. Children assist their parents in profound ways, aiding in the parents' growth and learning. Many parents would agree that they have developed many personal qualities and deeper understanding as a consequence of their interactions with their children. This comes about not only because of the discipline involved in caring for a child, but also because of the affecting presence of that particular child. Each educates the other. The underlying soul bond between them encourages learning and personal growth.

Sometimes my clients have described their influence upon the parents during the prenatal period. That influence has helped the parents to deal with problems that they scarcely could have resolved alone. Obviously, this assistance could not take the form of being helpful in a physical way. Rather, the prenatal infant, because of innate soul qualities and an inner connection of love with one or both of the parents, contributes an energizing force or harmonizing influence to them.

These infants enter the womb with already-developed positive qualities and strength of character which have a direct impact upon other family members. One such infant was Catherine, who combined the qualities of insight and positive energy. In her regression, Catherine said:

> *My father doesn't have the same need to spend as much time together as my mother does. When my mother gets upset, he listens and attends to what she says, but later he forgets and goes about his own activities.*
>
> *I love them both very much. I send them energy to help them come together. They feel it, even though they don't know that I am doing it. It works. I feel responsible for their relationship, but it's responsibility that I want to take, it's not a pressure.*

Now, as an adult, Catherine displays that same caring attitude and warmth toward others. She has an obvious charismatic quality of love. She is a manager in a business corporation, and is exceptional in her concern about the well-being of those whom she directs. It's easy to envision her as that unborn infant who expressed the good will that helped unify her parents.

A Sister Retains Her Hatred

Catherine's soul connection with her parents allowed her to project an energy that brought greater harmony to them. In an interesting deviation from the usual prenatal regression, my client Marsha's relationship to her sister—rather than her relationship to her mother—was the focus of our session. It appeared that the intensity of feeling between Marsha and her sister also indicated a soul connection. But this connection was a negative one. Marsha felt vulnerable to her sister's deep hostility.

Marsha began the regression by saying, "I can hear my sister shouting at my mother. She doesn't want my mother to be pregnant! My mother is very unhappy and upset at her shouting." With a little prompting to move on, she described the fourth month in the womb:

> *It's dark here. I can hear, but I can't see. I can hear my mother's thoughts! My mother is crying. She wants my sister to understand. My mother is so hurt, she so much wants another baby. She thought my sister would enjoy a brother or sister.*

As for her sister, Marsha said:

> *She brings flowers to my mother. My mother is taken in by the flowers. But there is hate in my sister's eyes. She is smiling in front, but there is hate in the back of her eyes.*

We moved ahead to the birth, which was comfortable and safe. But immediately afterwards there were problems with Marsha's sister. Marsha said, "Everyone is cooing at me, but my sister doesn't like it. To her, I am taking away her mother."

After her birth, Marsha had to find some way of dealing with her sister's hostility.

> *My sister pokes me with a pin when my parents are not close by. I am helpless! She is using me to get at my mother. I am confused because she uses me, but I also sense that she loves me. But I don't trust her. So I play with my stuffed animals and try to not get her attention.*

The rivalry between the sisters was not easily resolved. It persisted for many years, despite Marsha's natural desire to be on good terms with her sister. Only now, as adults, are the two sisters beginning to draw closer in a bond of affection.

In the next chapter we continue to investigate the deeper levels of our prebirth experience. We look into our experiences before conception, as we prepare to take a physical form. We explore our willingness to come to the earth to get born.

_13_

Coming to Earth

Laurie: "To make life happen, you have to get out of the corner and stop hiding! I can now say 'It's good to be here!' "

Transition

There is no question that emotional charges may be built up in the transition from spiritual being to human being. It is then that the soul adopts a human body, and there are powerful forces at work at this juncture. Some clients are happy to take on a physical form and enter this world, while others speak of their reluctance to leave their "home." For all of them, however, the actual transition from non-physical to physical form is a profound and sometimes traumatic experience.

Discontent at Leaving "Home"

My client, James, in his regression, showed an attitude of discontent right from the start. He said:

> *I would like to cry. I am being separated from something I so care about. It's the wholeness of the other dimension. I feel sorrow at being sent away. I'm told I will not be gone forever, that I will be returning, but I don't understand. I feel desolate to leave.*

And then:

I am resentful! This is the wrong place for me to be. I feel pressure and I am tense, and I don't want to be here!

Resistance to Being in the Physical World

My client, Laurie, spoke of her inner struggle about coming into a body:

> *To get born in the world I have to go into another physical body. I was trying to avoid that! I hate that sense of being confined in such a small space. I am numb and sad, knowing that I have to do this. A part of me is choosing it even while another part of me dislikes it. I feel like kicking and screaming!*

Yet another client, Carl, recalled this beginning to his prenatal period:

> *I am panicked! I want to go back, to turn back! I don't want to go in!*
>
> *I feel trapped, as though I am stuck. I can see the connection to the other side closing, diminishing. I can't turn back, and I know I have to stay here!*
>
> *I keep reminding myself that I wanted to be here, letting myself know that I'm strong enough to make it, that it's not the end.*
>
> *It's not a happy place here. Waves of negative feelings come over me—sadness, a lot of self-pity, and aloneness. It's confusing me. It's almost as though I'm drowning in a thick, weighty mass. There's a sense that the mass is not mine. It almost suffocates me! I can't wait to get out of here, to leave it behind. This is like being in a small chamber, and I have to endure it.*

The Effect of Resisting

Resistance to entering a physical body has been a frequent enough theme during my clients' regressions. This resistance to accepting the earth as a habitat, with its new opportunities and its new restrictions, often results in personal unhappiness. It seems intolerable to be here. Frequently, there is a sense of being victimized by life. The resistant individual lacks life goals, which ordinarily propel a person to engage in activities and to achieve satisfying results.

It is easy to see that by failing to be engaged in life, a person will also fail to be effective. The sense of purposelessness perpetuates itself, and there is no sense of deep satisfaction. Personal resistance to life, even with the best of motives, is in the long run unworkable. In time, the resistant person is confronted by life circumstances that force changes to come about, for something must be done when life becomes too difficult or unhappy.

The Psychology of Resistors

Just as children will ordinarily interpret their being badly treated by parents as due to some personal defect ("Daddy's angry—what did I do wrong?"), so too do some of those who are unhappy about being here interpret the very fact of having an earth life in a personal way. They will often take on a sense of inferiority. This inferiority is a natural consequence of interpreting this earth realm as inferior. The emotional logic is something like this: "Why would I, after all, be 'exiled' here to this inferior abode if I was not inferior or deserving of punishment? There must be something wrong with me, even if I am not sure what that is." I have speculated that this sense of inferiority might even be the original basis for the religious concept of "original sin."

To maintain themselves in the face of a hidden fear that they are inferior, and to survive in the uncongenial earth environment, these people often take on an attitude of spiritual superiority. They see themselves as having loftier ideals, visions, and concepts of how life should be lived than do others. They may believe that their mission in life is to enlighten others. This superiority is often given form by taking on a "spiritual" view of life, a view that defines ordinary physical experience as common and devoid of spirit. "Spiritual" values are seen as superior to the "worldly" values—such as money, power, or physical and sexual pleasures. They see others as lacking a worthwhile purpose in living. They, on the other hand, believe that they live spiritually, above all this, awaiting heavenly or other-worldly reward for all they have endured in being here. The reward is meant as compensation for the burdensome existence of enduring life in an inferior environment.

My work with them is designed to make them aware of their original resistance to physical life, and then of the special opportunities that earth life affords—opportunities to develop a sense of identity and to enable the energies of the soul and spirit to be manifested in the physical world through responsible and creative actions.

Longing for Unity

My client Laurie saw that the sense of "oneness" that she experienced during the regression, that sense of unity with the spiritual dimension, is what she has been longing for always. The big breakthrough in understanding came for Laurie at the end of our regression session, when she said:

> *I am admitting that I belong here on the earth. Some important inner part of me was denying that I could actually deal with the requirements here and take the responsibility. I made it harder by not taking responsibility. To make life happen, you have to get out of the corner and stop hiding! I can now say "It's good to be here!"*

I feel honored that I have been given the opportunity to assist clients in releasing their resistance to life, enabling them to recognize that they are really longing for their spiritual home. In the next chapter, we delve more deeply into the astonishing passage, which each of us has taken, in which we leave the spiritual dimension to become a human being in a courageous journey through life.

14

The Wheel of Life

Andrew: "I feel anticipation; another life is going to start!"

Before We Live on Earth

I have sometimes been led into unchartered territories by my clients. One such area is the non-physical dimension in which we exist before we make our journey into this physical world. The accounts of my clients' experiences prior to entering the womb are intriguing and thought provoking.

Here is what Andrew reported:

> *I am floating and am not physical. I have an awareness of being with others. I do not communicate with them, but we have an awareness of one another. I am 'me' and they are 'they,' but we are not individuals as you ordinarily think of them—we are all one big entity together, like a big ball, just 'being.'*

Some people describe their journey to earth like a ride down a tunnel. Andrew described it like this:

> *I feel myself sucked out of the ball, being drawn to the earth. It is a rapid journey. Now I feel myself sliding into the womb—an exciting moment! I feel anticipation, another life is going to start!*

Non-Physical Guides—The Wise Ones

In reporting on their experiences in the prior dimension, many clients, like Andrew, describe other "beings." In some cases, these beings have the function of guiding others, acting as "spiritual guides." The belief that human beings are guided and assisted by conscious, intelligent entities from a non-physical dimension is widespread—it is present to some degree in almost every religion and every culture in the world. In Western cultures, this concept takes the form of guardian angels, who assist people when they are in need of help. This belief in non-physical beings has, for the most part, become more or less of a myth—something like Santa Claus, a story to pass on to children but which is not taken very seriously.

According to the reports that I've received, as well as the research of others, spiritual guides are a significant source of assistance and comfort to us, unaware though we may be of their presence. In the many regressions she conducted, Dr. Helen Wambach reported, "Sixty-eight percent of my subjects felt reluctant, anxious, or resigned to the prospect of living another lifetime....Only 26 percent of my subjects looked forward to the coming lifetime, many of these subjects reporting that they had planned carefully, and felt they would have help from the other dimension in achieving their goals in this life."

Some of my clients have been familiar with the concept of spiritual guides, and they were comfortable with that idea even before we began their regression; others knew nothing about it. Karen was one of my clients who, initially, was unfamiliar with such guides. She is a gentle, caring person who was eager, perhaps too eager to come to earth. Here is a brief excerpt from her report.

M: I'd like to have you start by going to that dimension in which you existed prior to coming to the earth. Describe to me the feeling that you have in that other place.

K: *There's a sense of urgency. I feel the presence—I don't understand this—of a couple of—not people, but beings. I feel them—I just know they're here.*

M: Can you describe them?

K: *I can't see their physical appearance, but I can sense them. One is very warm and nurturing. The other just seems to be a "watcher." The nurturing guide and I are of the same energy. At times, we're connected. I can feel our energy bonding together and becoming one, and then we separate and go on. Somehow I feel as though my guide is feminine. Are guides feminine?*

M: They certainly can be. Do the guides communicate with you?

K: *I feel I am being sent a reassurance, but, at the same time, they seem to be aware that it's going to be a rough journey. They think I'm being hasty.*

M: How are you being hasty?

K: *I just have an urgency about wanting to be earthbound.*

In contrast to Karen, my client Charles, an ex-Marine who had visited foreign shores, was an enthusiastic and experienced traveler in the inner world. This is how he described his experience with his guides:

> *I am in a special place, waiting until I will be born. I feel apprehensive. I am aware of the activity of others, helping me to prepare. They are standing by.*
>
> *They are my guides. Each guide is different. The main guide, wearing white or pastel, has a lot of wisdom. Another guide, who wears a red robe is a teacher, oriented toward action. He is more direct. The third guide is a female. I feel from her a gentleness, love, and empathy. She has a calming influence on me. She is like a mother, one who is there to comfort. The fourth guide is there to*

help in practical matters. He is in the background, checking things out. He's mechanical, dealing with the "nuts and bolts," and his interest is on the practical level of getting things accomplished.

Charles elaborated on the character of the guides:

They are very experienced, confident, and knowledgeable. They cooperate well with one another. They've lived many lives themselves, and have a knowledge of the earth based on experience. They've been away from the earth for a short time; long enough to understand and integrate their experience here.

I asked Charles how he felt in the presence of his guides. He said, "They give me a feeling of reassurance. I feel good with them. They will all stay with me after I am born. They are a supportive group." I then led Charles's attention to the new life experience for which he was being prepared. Charles said:

I feel their activity, helping me to prepare for this lifetime. I am apprehensive. They are all serious, telling me that my life will be difficult, a real shock. The main guide is cautioning me, telling me it will be real intense. He says that it will be trouble, but to hang in there. The teacher guide says "We are ready. Now is the time to go!"

A Purpose for This Lifetime

I asked Charles about the significance of this lifetime for him, and he responded with this information:

Yes, it seems as though it would be easy to lose a lot of ground if this life doesn't go right. I feel like I have to be careful and prepare well. There is a danger of a strong setback.

I have developed strongly in one area in previous lives, and I have to balance that out. I could easily slip into that mode again. I'm speaking about power and control.

The qualities that Charles had developed in his evolutionary progress are traditionally seen as the masculine qualities, expressive of identity and personal will. The effort to conquer or to achieve is an expression of the masculine energy, but that effort has often been undertaken at the expense of others. And it is easy to see that Charles, the former Marine, has been assertive and controlling.

Asserting one's self is needed in order to be a whole and complete human being. But a sense of connection with, and sensitivity toward, others is the other half of the equation. Each of us eventually learns to express ourselves in coordination with other human beings, not in opposition.

The interaction with the guides made clear to Charles what he needed to learn, his purpose for this life. He commented:

> *I need to learn the other side, the feminine aspect—sensitivity, acceptance, letting go. I need to learn to live life instead of trying to control it. If I had tapped into the old energy of power and control, it would have been difficult to break away from it. I need to balance it out. That's why I am here.*

Apprehensive about His Return to Earth

Charles went on to describe his feelings upon leaving the prior dimension:

> *I'm feeling nervous. I have this feeling that you get before you're ready to do some major thing—a feeling of apprehension. It's a gathering of energy, getting ready for a shock. I'm more than just a little uneasy. I know that it's going to be more stressful in that family. It's not like I'm really excited about it.*

As Charles prepared to begin a new life on earth, he recognized that his relationship with the guides would change. He said:

I am saying good-bye to my guides. I won't be in the same kind of communication with them. I'll be engrossed in my life. It's like when I was playing basketball in high school. I knew my friends were in the stands—but I couldn't talk to them because I was involved in the game.

The connection with his guides became less immediate to Charles as he established his connection with his future family:

Now I can feel my mother, my father, the house. I'm right in the middle of it. The connection with my guides has dissolved, as I was expecting. I definitely sense a transition from being with my guides to being with my family. Before, I was with my guides and my family seemed distant, far away. Then I made the transition. And now my family seems very real to me, and my guides are off in the distance.

Charles did have a difficult childhood, as his guides foresaw. His mother, due to her anger at all men, did not support or nurture her young male child. His parents separated when he was six years old, and his father committed suicide when Charles was an adolescent. As a result of his own hurt, Charles has become more sensitive and receptive to others. These are the qualities that are so important for his soul development.

At the same time, Charles seems to have worked hard to learn to use power and control in a balanced and effective way. One can imagine that his guides have congratulated themselves and breathed a collective sigh of relief!

Diana: A Loving Spirit

Diana was a "natural" at doing regression work, although she had not had any practice previous to seeing me. She had the ability to travel in consciousness to other dimensions with complete ease

and she required almost no preparation by hypnotic induction to
do so.

Following my usual procedure, I directed Diana to view her
experience at the beginning of the gestation period. But her mind
brought her to an even earlier time. She began speaking of making plans for a new lifetime on earth.

She said, "It was planned that I should come through. It is not
a surprise. I knew I was coming back, I was conscious of it."

Diana described a sort of "containment area" in which souls
who were waiting to be born on earth were prepared for birth.
She said:

> *I am in a yellow room without walls. It's a holding area. There are
> a number of souls here, with others behind me. I have no contact
> with the others—I'm just in the presence of other souls. We are
> aware of what we're doing here. It's like a silent meditation. We're
> all concentrating, waiting for the right moment to come in. I
> know who I will be born to. I am intent on what I have to do and
> where I am going.*

I asked Diana where she had been before she came to this
holding area. She answered:

> *I was briefed before I came here. What happens is this: You finish
> up with one life. You talk to these beings who help you. You see
> what you need to do next. These beings sit at a table across from
> you. They look everything over, tell you what your strong points
> are, what your hindrances are, what would be helpful or beneficial
> for you. You meditate on what is said.*

I asked Diana how long this process took. She explained,
"There are moments, but no time. There are just experiences." I
asked her to tell me more about these beings who were assisting
her. She said:

There is a council made up of two or three beings. They look very human and are males. One of them is very old with white hair and a beard. The others are not clear to me. They are good at what they do, but they aren't super-advanced cosmic beings. They do, however, know the earth very well. They know how the karmic wheel turns. They have all had earth lives, although they are no longer working in the human dimension themselves.

Lovingly, they evaluate you and your growth. They are not at all judgmental. Rather, they present everything to you, saying, "This is what you're working on and this would make you stronger. We feel this is the best. How do you feel?" They advise everyone who comes through, in order. The presentation is clear, to the point, not at all foggy.

Curious about their advice to Diana, I asked "What specifically are they saying to you?" Diana replied:

They say to me, "You have very strongly developed compassion, courage, and childlikeness. You already know quite a lot—you have inner wisdom and inner strength. It is easy for you to grasp abstract ideas. But you now have to learn how to love all things on earth, not just the comfortable things, before you go back to the One."

The guides' advice fit with what Diana had said in an earlier past life regression:

The earth seems so base. I didn't want to give up spiritual identity. I felt tremendous sadness in coming here. I want that other level of spiritual expression. I'd rather be where it is more harmonious, where limitations aren't set upon you.

The council's advice to Diana shows that they recognized her difficulty in adjusting to life on the earth. Sometimes beings such as Diana have great difficulty in accepting the conflict and pain of life here. They do not recognize that life on earth provides a special opportunity for personal development, and that the earth is a unique and most valuable dimension for learning. Diana said:

> *Every other time that I've been here until now has been very tough, and I have not accepted it. I was very stubborn. I wasn't going to change until I was good and ready. You don't change until the time is right!*

Diana further explained the council's recommendations to her before entering this life:

> *They stressed that I really needed to learn how to embrace it all, not just the "good." My fear would be my worst enemy, fear of what I think can hurt me, fear of what I think is bad. They said I have a lot of light—I have to be the master of it. Instead, I'm letting my fear control it. I feel vulnerable in a physical form!*

A Life or Death Choice

After we had discussed the "briefing" and advice of the council, Diana went on to describe her transition from that dimension to the earth.

> *It's like in-between. I'm starting to lose memory—I can't quite remember where I was before, but I don't quite know where I'm going, either! There is a lot of white light around. It's very quiet, very peaceful.*

Following this transitional phase, Diana provided a vivid description of her experience before the moment of conception and of how she bonded with the fertilized egg. She said:

> *That's when I was a little spark, the spark right before the process of conception begins. I was this little spark of light, like an electron or atom. I'm all compacted into this tiny spark, inside the womb at the time of conception. My consciousness is right there. What a trip!*

I asked Diana what happened to the spark at the time of conception. She explained:

My consciousness is in the spark; the spark is inside the womb at the time of conception. That's where I'm placed. I'm surrounded by white, billowy air, yet I'm in the womb.

Diane continued her description of the changes occurring after conception. She reported that:

As the cells are dividing more and more, I get more and more into the physical. It seems like a very gradual process. The white light is diffusing into all the cells that are dividing. As the process continues, everything becomes more dense. I feel kind of like I'm suspended in a void. My point of focus is changing—it's becoming much more "here and now."

As Diana became more invested in her physical body, she became more sensitive to her environment. She said:

My body is forming, I am floating around. There are a lot of loud sounds. I get a quick passing sense of anger all around me. It's scary! I'm having a hard time staying here. It seems really scary.

It was too frightening for Diana's sensitive system to accommodate. She said,

I couldn't stay, it was just too much. It's almost like my nervous system just couldn't handle it! I just withdrew, I don't even know where I went. I just wanted it to be quiet really badly! So I ran, kind of like I was escaping.

Diana was unclear about her experience after she left the body, so I directed her to go to the point at which she once again felt associated with the developing fetus. She said:

I didn't settle back in again until the very end [of the pregnancy]. I came and went earlier, but I wasn't wanting to stay for very long. I was just "in" and "out." I was really there to stay only towards the very end, about the last month and a half.

Musing on her return to the womb, Diana said:

It's funny. I had a choice before I came back during the eighth month—I could have tried to vacate. I had to make a choice at about seven months. Up until that time, I had been coming and going, not real invested in the body. It was all or nothing by the eighth month. I chose to stick with it. It seems as though when you go into the physical, you have to let go of everything else, you have to totally commit to it. It just took me a little bit longer to do that.

It was up to me whether I wanted to be born or not. It was totally my choice. I had to make the decision and commitment, focussing all my energy and concentration and will on that. It was up to me and I decided to really go for it!

Suppose you had not? I asked. Diana replied:

The body would not have formed and I would have left, and gone back. If I had decided to pull out, the body would have died. It was developing during the months I was "out," but the development was slower than it would have been. At the time that I decided to stay, I decided to really connect with the body and make sure that it survived. I was determined. That's the way I was feeling.

Her decision to remain and be born focussed her attention on the life awaiting her. "Part of me is excited that I have this opportunity! I am really looking forward to it," said Diana. She continued:

I have an opportunity at life, at fully realizing the best it can be. I am so hopeful and idealistic! This might really be a chance to make things wonderful. I am really determined to do my best!

Hearing her zeal and enthusiasm, I asked Diana what she wanted to accomplish in the life to come. She responded by saying:

I want it to be the best it can be here, [to be a place] where people live in cooperation and reach their full potential. I want to be the best I can be so that the world really works! Everything works when people are happy—rather than fighting and in chaos, feeling

*all the heartache and loneliness that people feel. If I can bring
more light in, it might help.*

So Diana decided to participate in life in a physical body on earth, and to assist others as an expression of her love and idealism. Her sincerity was obvious. She determined to not be frightened by the harshness of life, nor would she be likely to act "spiritually" superior to others.

As we continued, we focussed on the effect that Diana's critical decision had upon the development of the fetus during the eighth month of the gestation. She said:

*I can feel everything, my body is so sensitized. I can feel myself
expanding and growing, and I can feel blood flowing up and down
the spine—that's where everything is really happening. My spine
is expanding and I feel energy flowing into my arms, legs and
head. Energy is coursing through my body.*

She had bravely decided to remain and to contribute to the betterment of others. And yet we see in the regression transcript that follows that this sensitive being needed all her will and determination to survive. She had made a decision, but implementing it on the physical level of life proved extremely strenuous for her. She was strongly affected by her parents. She described her efforts in our regression dialogue:

M: Are you sensitive to the outer circumstances?

D: *Yes, the chaos is still there, but I am determined. I am almost mad!
I am going to be born and am not going to let those impressions
affect me as much!*

M: Are you aware of your mother?

D. *I am aware of my mother's love. That's one of the factors that
helped me decide to stay. It's as though she and I made an agreement. She has a lot of love and I want to stay.*

My mother really does want this baby. She really wants another child. [There were two older brothers.] I feel a sense of protection and a lot of love from her. She's happy to be pregnant.

The sounds I was so sensitive to before were from my dad. I don't know exactly what was going on, but it was too much for me!

M: What is your mother's feeling toward your father?

D: *She feels a lot of anger and a lot of pain. They are not in a good relationship. They love each other but they are just not getting along. There's a lot of fighting and a lot of yelling. I'm not really in touch with my dad at all.*

I don't like the fighting at all! Earlier in the pregnancy, I had felt too fragile to handle the fighting. Now that I have more of a body, I am able to handle it better. Plus, I am just determined to get born. It's really up to me.

The Infant Knows Better than the Doct When to Get Born

M: What's happening as the birth approaches?

D: *I am growing, becoming more and more cramped.*
all the space there is. I feel very heavy, very dens̄   ̄ed
down. I am concentrating on how I am going   I'm
putting my concentration on getting ou'   ̄t of
focus.

My mother told me that I was born a   doctor
was concerned. But according to my book   on time!
When I got back into the body at eight mon   develop-
ing as it should. "Oh, oh, I'd better get or   ," I said to
myself. There was rapid development in   Sudden-
ly, I got energized and I took off.

At nine months, I was developed ̄   have sur-
vived. But I would have been very si   ll. I had to

really push to get up to weight and size that would be okay, so I could hold my own after birth. I went from fairly dense to really dense in the last month. My will and presence helped the body to grow.

M: How did your mother feel about your being overdue?

D: *She was very patient about it all. She didn't worry or anything. She figured I'd come in my own good time.*

Good Thinking Assists the Birth

M: Let's move ahead to the birth.

D: *I was thinking about how I would get out of here. I put my head down. I figured it out, that's the way you do it. I was analytical even back then! I just started putting my weight there so it would happen. I was real anxious to get born. Things were moving all around me. I was rather tense, directing all my energy and concentration into making this work.*

It's pretty scary trying to get through this birth! Things are swooshing around me, water, everything. It seems to take forever. All of a sudden everything's changing, almost like a giant earthquake.

My head peeps out—it's bright! I went from dark to light. It seems to take a long time to get through—yet at the same time, it's real fast. After I get pulled out, I stay watching everything from outside the body.

M: How is your mother feeling?

D: *My mom is real happy, smiling and laughing. I get a sense of her joy. I am just a little scrawny red thing, bawling my eyes out!*

Fright at Being Separated

D: *All of a sudden it's real scary. They are handing me around, poking things in me. All of a sudden, I am in this chaos. It's colder and foreign.*

Suddenly I'm no longer with my mom. I'm scared! Where did she go? They are taking me away. I am crying, I want to stay with her. There is separation everywhere. This is not what I was expecting!

My emotions are like a roller coaster! At first I had felt exhilaration at being born, then comes this fear, feeling so alone and abandoned.

Later, I get back to my mom. I know who she is! She's different from all the other moms. I'm okay when I'm with her, I can rest. When they take me away from my mom, I know I'm not going to be harmed, but it's just too scary! I don't want to be away from her at this time.

M: Is your dad there?

D: *Yes, my dad is smiling at me, trying to make me laugh. I get a sense of love from him. He's real happy. I know who he is, but I don't know him the way I know my mother.*

The Guides Save Diana's Life

We continued by examining the early months after Diana's birth. Diana had made a decision in the womb to be born. However, her resistance to life on earth had again been triggered, perhaps by the harsh experiences following her birth. Whatever the cause, her reaction against being here surfaced again and she described the situation this way:

When I was three months old, I tried to get out of being here. I got really sick with bronchitis. I wanted out really bad! Left to my own devices, I would have died then.

Diana saw that several spiritual guides came to her rescue at that time. She said:

Higher beings—from where I was before I decided to be born—assisted me, working in conjunction with my higher self to keep me in the physical level. I remember them all around my body. I was in an air tent. They directed a lot of energy to me. I could feel it coming into me. That kept me going.

And so she is here now, a person with much love and spiritual awareness to share with us. Even now she is learning to accept and benefit from life on earth and to integrate her experiences here with those experiences of harmony and love she has known in another dimension. We are most fortunate to have this sweet young person here.

Possibilities and Speculations

This chapter, and the previous one, have dealt with awareness before physical life, and awareness of entering physical life. The excerpts of regressions that I have included open up endless possibilities for further inquiry. What is the scope of our soul's journey before birth and after death? In the following chapter, I reflect on the larger meaning of my clients' experiences.

_15_

Dimensions of Consciousness

We are dealing here with the concept of a continuity of consciousness—the idea that we are in the process of personal evolution as we pass through various realms of existence.

After more than fifteen years of guiding individuals through prenatal regression, the merits of the process and the validity of prebirth experiences and memories are, for me, no longer in question. As you have shared the experiences presented in this book, I cannot help but believe that you, if not convinced, will at least be open to the possibility.

Continuity of Consciousness

It would seem that we are conscious both before birth and after death, and that our awareness is not dependent upon our residence in a physical body. We are dealing here with the concept of a continuity of consciousness—the idea that we are in the process of a personal evolution as we pass through various realms of existence. It implies that we are a small part of an evolving universe and that our personal evolution has a correspondence with the pattern of universal evolution.

Our awareness, or state of consciousness, changes as we experience the different dimensions of life. When we inhabit the higher spiritual dimensions, where we exist without a physical body, we have a particular outlook or perspective. An impressive shift comes about when we enter the prenatal period, and the influence of the emotions predominate. And yet, despite the diversity of our experience, there is a continuity of experience in the successive realms of life. The experiences in one realm can profoundly affect the next.

An example of this continuity appears in the transition into a prenatal body. Our prenatal experience is often significantly influenced by our earlier experiences in the spiritual dimensions of life.

Beliefs About Life Before Conception

I have worked with people who have a very wide range of backgrounds and beliefs, ranging from strict Catholic to Zen Buddhist. Their belief systems often did not include a recognition or acceptance of the idea of being conscious before becoming human. Nevertheless, despite the diversity of backgrounds, I found a consistency in their responses. They were describing an unfamiliar area of experience, something about which they may never have given any thought, and yet their descriptions were quite similar.

Before Birth and After Death

The reports I received are consistent with those given by Dr. Raymond Moody, a physician, in his widely read book *Life After Life*. His book describes near-death experiences, and gives the reports of a number of people who were designated as medically dead. They tell of leaving their bodies and going to a non-physical dimension in which they experienced a sense of release, freedom, and harmony. They speak of receiving assistance from others beings, beings who expressed an elevated quality of love and wisdom. And they returned to our physical dimension and continued to live, with memories that were most comforting and that some-times changed the course of their lives.

My clients report existing in a comparable environment before they came into our physical realm. Both Dr. Moody's reports and mine indicate a continuity of consciousness. His reports show that a person retains awareness after the death of the body; my reports show that a person is also aware before coming into a body. The traditional idea of going to heaven after death implies a similar continuity of consciousness from the physical to the non-physical dimensions, although nothing specific seems to be said in the tra-ditional Western religious literature about awareness before incar-nation. However, in the traditional Eastern religions, Hinduism and Buddhism, the belief in reincarnation is supported by reli-gious texts that describe the stages of transition between death in one life and birth into another. In *The Tibetan Book of the Dead*, these stages are called "bardos," and they define the different levels of consciousness that accompany the successive stages.

The issue of past lives takes us into a controversial area. The controversy, however, centers on the fact that we are here probing an area that cannot be scientifically quantified. Still, as I have worked in this area over the years, I have witnessed hundreds of people, many of them skeptics, who found themselves encounter-ing vivid memories of other lives during their sessions. What seems particularly useful from such sessions is that these past life experiences mirror and make sense of issues that these people are experiencing in the present. Common themes may be echoed from a past life into the current one. New insights and under-standings that ensue help the person resolve problems that previ-ously had seemed unsolvable.

Though it may be a surprise to some Westerners, the majority of the world's population holds a belief in reincarnation. Even here in the West, a Gallup poll taken of the American adult population in 1981 showed that 23 percent believe in reincarnation. This is a high percentage, considering that reincarnation goes against the prevailing cultural beliefs. These results are comparable to other polls taken in Europe. In Asia, where Buddhism and Hinduism are the most popular religions, the belief in reincarnation is predominant. It is a belief that answers questions often asked about the inequalities between human beings. It suggests that the current life of each individual is, at least in part, determined by what has been done in past lives.

In recent years there has been an upsurge of interest in ancient texts of cultures more spiritually oriented than our own. There has also been a great deal of interest in integrating spiritual knowledge with psychology. Out of this marriage between ancient and modern, we've begun to create some very fruitful and gratifying ways of delving into the mystery of our lives. Whether we call this area of study "psycho-spiritual psychology," "transpersonal psychology," "holistic studies," "consciousness research," or by one of the various other names we use to label this work, we are seeing an expanding field that is drawing professionals from all over the world.

For those with open minds this is a vast and rich territory, one that has already proven to be of immeasurable benefit to thousands of people. Our deeper understanding of the spiritual dimensions of our lives brings to light avenues of awareness through which we can improve our individual lives and, in the process, contribute to the creation of a better world.

16

Recommendations for Parents

What, I have reflected, is the best advice I can offer you when you are pregnant? What will best serve the child that you will parent? It may sound strange, but I would say that the best gift you can give your infant is to LOVE YOURSELF. That is, however, not always easily accomplished! All too many of us are critical and demanding of ourselves—often much harsher than we are of others. We would benefit greatly from being on good terms with ourselves, and so would our unborn infants.

Loving yourself will allow you to better love your child, and will allow your child to better love himself. Be kind to yourself. That seems like the most important of all the rules, for our attitudes in life are so affected by our self-love. Pregnancy has its joys, but it also may take much effort and patience, and can be burdensome. Loving yourself will assist in creating the environment of love so nurturing to your child.

Secondly, recognizing your soul connection with your unborn infant enriches your relationship with him. And recognizing that your infant is aware of you, and is sensitive to your feelings and thoughts—even more sensitive than you may be—can change the way you relate to him.

Communicating With the Unborn Infant

How can you develop a relationship with your unborn infant? Many women talk and sing to the infant in their womb, instinctively communicating and bonding with their child. These mothers, strong in their instinctual abilities, feel an inner connection with the infant they are carrying. They sense the feelings of the infant in the womb and transmit their own feelings and thoughts to him. These mothers sometimes know at the very moment that it happens, that they have conceived.

An excellent way to develop greater sensitivity to the infant, and to better communicate with him, is to use the following visualization process: Sit quietly with your eyes closed for a few minutes, move into a relaxed state; then imagine that the spirit of your unborn child is in front of you. Feel his presence, and take the time needed to sense each another. Speak to your infant, express your feelings and share your experiences. Be aware of and communicate the love you feel for this soul that has come to be your child. Take the time to sense a response from your infant. That response may be a feeling or a thought that comes to your mind. Ask him what is important to him and what he would like from you. Like many other parents who have done this, you might be quite surprised by the answers.

Then imagine you are experiencing the light of his soul. Perhaps you have an impression of light emanating from this being. Talk to this soul. Ask questions; then *trust* the impressions and answers that come to you.

Sometimes you cannot tell if you have a boy or girl, but you will notice a pronounced quality that characterizes that being, a distinct, essential nature. That quality may seem predominantly male or predominantly female, reflecting a quality of character but not necessarily sexual identity. (How many women do you know that were sure of the gender of their child, only to be surprised at birth?)

Develop a sensitivity to the personality of your unborn. Some infants are peaceful in nature, some are vigorous, some emotional, some independent, some needy and dependent. Infants have their own intrinsic personal qualities. Take careful note of the nature of your unborn infant. Your recognition contributes to his developing sense of identity. It sends him a message that his nature is distinct from others.

As you continue your interaction, your sensitivity will increase and you will feel the quality and energy of the unborn soul with increasing clarity. If you have not done this exercise before, let me emphasize that it may take some repetitions to feel certain about your experiences. In his book *Communing With the Spirit of Your Unborn Child,* Dawson Church agrees: "As we begin to tune in to a baby, our perceptions may be faint and indistinct at first, but will become more precise with use. We aren't given much scope for developing these sensitivities as we grow up so we tend to grow up without them. The advent of a new baby is a great opportunity to begin to develop our faculties of spiritual perception. And this sensitivity will allow our baby to communicate its needs to us."

To enhance your ability to relate to your unborn, I recommend two books. Dawson Church's book, *Communing With the Spirit of Your Unborn Child,* describes the "Radiance Method" of communicating with and sending positive energy to the unborn infant in the womb. This book provides a spiritual perspective on the nature of the parent-child relationship and contains meditations and exercises to enhance that relationship. Another excellent book along these same lines is *Nurturing the Unborn Child,* by Dr. Thomas Verny and Pamela Weintraub. This book provides a comprehensive nine-month program, using contemporary techniques, including visualizations, dream work, music, partner dialogue, affirmations, tactile stimulation and other tools designed to create inner harmony and bonding with the unborn infant.

Building a Relationship
With Your Unborn Child

As parents, we feel both love and a deep sense of responsibility for our infants. We recognize the infant's dependence on us, for even two years after birth toddlers are only beginning to walk and feed themselves. We humans remain dependent on our parents longer than virtually any animal; most animals can fend for themselves relatively soon after birth.

This intimacy of an unborn infant with the mother gives her a unique opportunity to help her infant. The preborn needs an environment that is nurturing and harmonious. He needs love, recognition, and acceptance. It is important that you, as parents, recognize that the preborn is a real person, a human being who has the awareness necessary for bonding with you, even though you have not heard his voice, looked into his eyes, or held him. The key to harmonious and loving relationships of any kind is communication. Let your baby know you love him. That will be a blessing to him.

Let your infant get to know you as a person, with all your strengths and limitations. This may take some courage, but it is so helpful to not hide. Communicate your feelings to the infant. We adults often enough become angry, hurt, or otherwise emotionally affected by events surrounding us. It is important to tell your infant that your negative feelings are not caused by him, that he is not at fault and should not blame himself. We have seen throughout this book how easily the unborn infant misunderstands. Talk to your infant each day when you are relaxed, and explain what you are feeling and going through, so that he knows that he is not personally causing the problems.

Emotions are often heightened when pregnancy occurs, whether the pregnancy was desired or not. We are concerned about how the birth will affect our lives. So much of importance is affected—the relationship with our spouse, our children and friends, the family budget, and our career. Ideally, for the peace of all, these concerns should be resolved as quickly as possible and the unborn child accepted and welcomed. Yet many of us who have gone through a pregnancy know how much more easily this is said than done! Communication with the unborn is especially critical under these trying circumstances. Do your best to lovingly share your dilemmas, your feelings, and your understanding. Communicate with your unborn infant so that instead of feeling isolated, he bonds in understanding more closely with you.

As you continue developing the relationship with the newly arrived soul in your womb, you can also assist him in other ways. For example, since the unborn infant cannot control his environment—he cannot change his circumstances—he may mistakenly assume that painful situations are permanent, and that a mother's temporary unhappiness or physical distress is an unchanging condition. This is characteristic of unborn infants. When you explain that experiences change, that emotional pain and physical distress pass, and that he can look forward to future happiness, you are providing him with a more comforting and knowledgeable adult perspective.

But keep it simple. Try to assist your unborn child to understand the immediate situations of life. Don't emphasize experiences that are beyond his range, such as the complexities of the workplace or political events, for these might be confusing. You can, however, speak of the brothers and sisters that await him, of family interactions and even difficulties you are having adjusting to his coming, always making certain that you make it clear that he is not to blame for these problems and that you or other adults will take responsibility for finding solutions.

As the time approaches, you might discuss the birth process and the new interaction that you and he will develop after his birth, when he is no longer inside your body. You might want to describe how he will be fed—by nursing or a bottle, and who will do it—how he will be kept safe and warm—not by mother's body but by clothing, a soft bed, a warm room—how he will receive love—people will hold him, hug him—and how he will begin perceiving a new, vast world through his five senses.

Special Problems

In contemporary life, the issue of abortion—natural and induced—has been spotlighted. Politics aside, it is important to recognize our responsibility to communicate with the preborn infant when he is not carried to full term for any reason. In her book, *Found, A Place for Me,* Sandra Landsman has observed that "When a woman knows at conception that she is pregnant, as many do, and decides that she unequivocally does not want the baby, she can cause a spontaneous abortion."

When parents feel that they are not able to go through with the pregnancy, and they are planning a medical abortion—often a difficult, emotional decision forged under stressful conditions—it is especially important that the reasons for the termination of pregnancy be expressed through an inner dialogue with the soul of the unborn. I have known several people who have done this. They reported that a spontaneous abortion occurred, that the infant's soul left the body. And very importantly, they sensed that the unborn soul left with understanding and acceptance. There always remains the possibility that the soul will be reborn to the same parents at a later time because of the strong inner bond that initially drew them together.

Whether the parents are delighted by the pregnancy, surprised by it, dismayed and making an effort to adjust, or are under such pressure that they feel an abortion is their only choice, it is an act of love for the parents to communicate with the conscious infant in the womb.

Healing Miscarriage, Stillbirth, and Abortion Experiences

I work with clients who have had a miscarriage, stillbirth, or an abortion earlier in life. Some of them still feel grief, regret, or guilt, and have not fully realeased these emotions. They had not known, at the time of their loss, that they could communicate with the infant they had lost and by doing so bring about resolution, healing and inner peace.

I find that this communication can still be established many years after the loss. It is never too late to improve the situation and to bring emotional healing to both the adult and the soul that was not born.

The process of communication is similar to the one described earlier in this chapter, in the section *Communicating With the Unborn Infant*. Follow the same directions given about how to get in touch with the soul of the unborn being, and when you feel yourself in connection with the soul of the infant, express your feelings to that soul—express your grief over the loss, or your reasons for not continuing the pregnancy if you had an abortion. Share your feelings and allow your love to be expressed. At the same time, be receptive to the responses of the soul with whom you are communicating. Perhaps that soul had his own reasons for not being born, reasons that relate to health, emotions, gender or other conditions.

Here is an opportunity to let go of the guilt, grief or regret that has affected you. Working with this process can lead to a deeper understanding of why the situation occurred and an acceptance of the uncompleted pregnancy. This process may bring understanding and a bond of enduring love between you and that other soul.

Some Final Words of Advice

Birthing Practices

The environment of childbirth is affecting to both mother and infant. In the past, medical practices have been based on the view that newborns are not aware and do not remember their birth. A mother's emotional connection with her newborn was overlooked in preference to standards of efficiency and cleanliness. There was no awareness of the need for fathers to be sharing the experience of the birth, to comfort and support their wives or partners, and to nurture and welcome their newborn babies.

Fortunately, in the past few years, new childbirth practices have been adopted that better suit the sensitivity of both mother and infant. Comfortable, attractive birthing rooms are now provided in some hospitals, and fathers can be present at the birth and may assist in it. Natural childbirth, with its techniques that provide comfort to the mother and to the newborn infant, have been introduced by pioneers such as Dr. Frederick Leboyer, author of *Birth Without Violence*. No longer are the newborns to be shocked by the cold temperatures and bright lights of the delivery room. Going a step further, some birthing centers provide water births to ease the transition of the newborn. In this process the child is born into warm water, providing an environment similar to the one in the womb, where he had been bathed in amniotic fluids.

Using Prenatal Regressions

My experience with prenatal regression therapy indicates that it is highly beneficial if completed before a woman conceives. When a woman becomes pregnant, the emotional and physical changes that occur usually trigger a subconscious response to her own experiences in the womb. At a deep level, her body remembers, and a flood of emotions and memories may be released.

As an example, I can point out the experience of a friend of mine, a lawyer and the father of an adopted daughter. At the age of eighteen the daughter became pregnant while away at college. However, she avoided telling her adoptive parents because she feared that they would urge her to have an abortion. She gave birth to the baby and immediately gave her up for adoption—as she herself had been given up years earlier. When they learned of this, her own adoptive parents were sorrowful; they would have wanted her to keep the child. However, her own experience in being adopted had been so intense that she was subconsciously impelled to repeat the experience in her adult life.

How many times have we heard of this sort of thing happening? Statistics show that many child abusers were themselves abused children, evidence that body memory patterns sometimes prove more powerful than good intentions. Particular life experiences trigger the subconscious memories of earlier experiences and they are played out again, although in different roles.

Because these deep-seated body memories can be so determinative, I suggest that women who anticipate becoming pregnant may benefit greatly from reexperiencing their own gestation. A regression would help release hidden, sometimes highly influential memories. Resolving prenatal wounds would help women develop greater self-love and self-esteem. And, they would gain greater empathy with the experiences of their own unborn infant.

However, I recommend that women already pregnant should not make use of prenatal regression therapy except in special circumstances, since the process may prove emotionally unsettling or may adversely affect the unborn infant. The issues that concern them can be resolved through prenatal regression work after the child is born.

Words for Parents

Whenever I finish a lecture on some of the material that has been presented in this book, the room becomes quiet and intense. The unspoken thoughts of parents in the audience run along these lines: "I can see that I really messed up during the pregnancy and I hurt my child." Feelings of guilt and regret are frequently expressed. Some parents judge themselves quite harshly.

Yet looking at these people, I see human beings, just like you and me. We all wish we were able to live our ideals, but life is filled with stressful times, and we go through them as well as we are able. It is natural in hindsight to berate ourselves. Yet it seems so important to be compassionate toward the person that we were at that time, to be understanding and forgiving. The path to self-acceptance and self-love may not be easy. Can we be as loving toward ourselves as we would be toward a person going through experiences similar to ours?

Ironically, if you had been a "better" parent you might not have been parent to your child. I believe that infants and parents are joined together in relationships which assist in our personal growth and evolution. Soul choices are not random. Children and parents are drawn together to learn through both "positive" and "negative" experiences, and our imperfections, as well as our desirable qualities, do in some sense contribute to the growth and development of our loved ones.

Some parents, exposed to these ideas, have spoken to their children about the stressful or emotional conditions they experienced during the pregnancy. This provides them with a greater understanding of their early life influences and facilitates their further growth. But all sharing must be done in a way that is appropriate to the child or adolescent involved.

Learning from Your Unborn Infant

The case histories in this book encourage us to recognize and respect unborn infants and to relate to them as souls—individuals who do not have mastery over the use of their bodies, but who are, nevertheless, highly aware of, and sensitive to, their experiences.

Many religious traditions state that babies have a special holiness, a special closeness to God. In this sense, an infant may be more aware of some dimensions of life than we adults. While it is true that the infant learns from us how to develop skills and abilities for getting along in the physical world, it is also true that the infant can teach us about our own spiritual origins. The child reminds us that as souls we, too, have a purpose for being here; that our purpose guides the experiences of our life, determines who our parents and friends will be, who we will marry, and yes, who our children will be.

What a difference it can make in our lives to recognize the infant as our teacher! Our relationship to a child takes on a more profound significance. From this perspective a parent might ask different questions, questions such as, "Why is this infant soul in my life?" The parent might ask not only "What may I do for this infant?" but also "What is this infant able to teach me?" Whether you are the natural parent, the adopting parent, the grandparent, or even a friend of the family, ask yourself, "What special attraction brought this child to enter my life?"

It is not unusual to hear from expectant mothers that being pregnant is a profound experience, an experience of participating in the cosmic forces of life. Pregnancy takes the mother, and sometimes the father, beyond the personal and familiar world of everyday life. This is a time of heightened sensitivity, when the pregnant woman is living at the crossroads of two worlds, the physical and the spiritual. In addition to bearing a child, giving birth has a subtler and broader meaning, and that is to release some part of the Greater Life, or God, onto the earth. At this time the mother will tap new, deeper, and more profound springs of life through this blessed mystery.

For the father, participating in giving the seed from which life sprang, participating as an initiator of life, it is a time of deep pride—a time to take on greater engagement and responsibility in life, and in the life of his child. Fathers can become highly sensitive to the soul of their unborn infant, and should be encouraged to join in this process.

Vision

It is my hope that, having read this book, you will not look at an infant in a limited way again. No longer need you limit your relationship to the infant to that of an adult with a scarcely sentient cub. This new outlook can assure us that newborns are cared for and nurtured as the very sensitive, dependent human beings that they are. This book is meant to encourage this approach and to give substance to what has been evident to the observant—that we are deeply affected by all of our early experiences and that we require special care and nurturing in our very vulnerable condition before, during, and immediately after birth.

The untarnished and endearing beauty of the newborn is more than physical. The face we look at still shines with the light of that everlasting realm from which we ourselves came, and shows us who we truly are—we who have become enmeshed in the world and forgotten ourselves. As the great English poet William Wordsworth wrote in his poem "Intimations of Immortality":

> ...*trailing clouds of glory do we come*
> *From God, who is our home:*
> *Heaven lies about us in our infancy!*
>
> ODE: INTIMATIONS OF IMMORTALITY
> FROM RECOLLECTIONS OF EARLY CHILDHOOD

Appendix A

The Nature and Functioning of the Prenatal Infant

You will find below a summary of the primary aspects of the prenatal condition. These generalizations may not speak for all prenatal infants, but they do provide us with some reference points that can help us focus on the nature of life before birth.

1. In the womb, we do not have a sense of self. We have not yet developed a separate identity or autonomy.

2. We are receptive, or reactive, to the emotions and energies of our mother, the environment in which we live. We do not initiate actions through the exercise of our will or determination.

3. We tend to empathetically absorb the mother's, and occasionally the father's, emotions.

4. We have little ability to distinguish between the feelings of others and our own feelings.

5. We have no way to escape or distance ourselves from emotions that we find unpleasant or threatening. We are vulnerable to the parental emotions that encompass us.

6. We have no psychological skills for deflecting, containing, modifying, or releasing negative emotions.

7. We have little sense of time and the process of change. We do not recognize that experiences change, cease, or are replaced by other experiences. The present moment, joyous or painful, seems eternal.

8. Within our limited capacities, we adapt to the prenatal environment. Our emotions, attitudes, self-esteem and self-expression are given definition by these adaptations to our prenatal experience, and following birth our psychological development is strongly influenced by them.

Appendix B

Psychological Adaptations During Gestation

An infant in the womb is extremely open and sensitive to the energies that encompass her. She may experience her environment as joyous or traumatic, depending on the quality of feeling she receives from her mother. She is ordinarily deeply affected by the mother's emotional, mental, and physical state.

She does not have a sense of being a separate individual, of having a separate identity. As a result, she does not recognize the difference between her mother's experiences and her own experiences. "When mother is unhappy, that is how I feel" is commonly reported during prenatal regressions.

For instance an infant responds to the emotional energy of an unhappy mother. Her reactions are experienced at a fundamental level, as body responses, rather than thoughts. She then forms an adaptation to the unpleasant atmosphere that envelopes her. This adaptation provides a way of coping with her mother's emotional energies. Depending on her predisposition, she may adapt in one of various ways: by pulling back and becoming overly self-reliant, recognizing that her mother is not available to support her; by deciding to emotionally and physically assist her mother after birth; or by reacting against her mother, and, after birth, focusing her attention toward her father. Or she may choose still another adaptation.

The adaptations will often strongly influence the emotional patterning and personality development following birth. As the infant matures into adulthood, she develops a more complex personality, a defined structure for responding to life experiences and for initiating actions. She becomes more individualized and develops her sense of self. Nevertheless, she frequently contains at her core the primal emotions associated with her intense experiences while in the womb. The prenatal infant self remains influential in the adult.

I have listed below five significant adaptations that I have found to be common among prenatal infants:

1. Becoming Self-Reliant

An adaptation made by some prenatal infants, ordinarily those who have not received nurturing from their mother, and lack the feeling of being protected by her, is to take responsibility for themselves, even to the extent that they sometimes become aggressively self-reliant. These infants do not have a feeling of being in a supportive, caring world, and so strive to confront life through their own isolated efforts. This adaptation is illustrated in greater detail in Chapter 4, "No One to Rely on but Herself."

2. Assuming Responsibility for Parents

An adaptation that other unborn infants make is to take responsibility for the distressed or burdened parent(s), making an inner commitment to assist them. The infant is prompted by empathy. On a more subtle level, she is also prompted by her survival instinct, since she needs her parents to survive. Often, these infants feel a sense of guilt for burdening the parent(s).

After birth, some infants actively help their parents by emotionally supporting them, trying to keep them from being distressed. Others, more passive, become "good children." They restrain themselves so that they are untroublesome and well-behaved. The pattern often carries into adulthood, when these people seek out others to "rescue." This adaptation is illustrated in Chapter 5, "Assuming Responsibility for the Parents."

3. Withdrawing from Life into Safety

In contrast, some infants may do the very opposite and withdraw from parents and life into an inner isolation. They separate themselves from the emotional currents of the family. Although they do succeed in cutting themselves off from distressing emotions, the positive emotions of love, nurturance, and belonging are cut off as well. Many of these infants become adults who live in their minds, poorly connected with the life energies of the body—energies of love, expressiveness, sexuality, creativity, etc. For them, the world of emotions and feelings is a foreign one. Often without even knowing or fully registering it, they live in deprivation and they lack loving relationships. This adaptation is illustrated in Chapter 6, "A Retreat from Life."

4. Selective Response

A fourth response consists of rejecting the specific source of pain. For example, an unborn infant may reject the unloving mother and form an emotional alliance with the father. This rejection may later become generalized; thus, a son who rejected his mother may become an adult who is distrustful and disconnected from all women. This adaptation is illustrated in Chapter 7, "Some Choose Sides and Some Choose Success."

5. Compensatory Responses

When conditions in the womb are difficult, the unborn infant may adapt by making a compensatory response. An example of such a response would be a determination to become successful in life. This adaptation enables the infant to maintain a forward-moving, extroverted energy, rather than becoming closed down or introverted. When young, those who have adapted this way often strive to get good grades in school; later they seek recognition through professional status. However, a fragile self-esteem often underlies their drive for achievement. Their self-worth is conditional, dependent upon success.

There are other forms of compensation, as well. I have shown that in cases where children are not of the gender desired by their parents, they may try to compensate by developing the kind of personality their parents might want them to have. Others in like circumstances choose a different adaptation, such as emotionally withdrawing from an unaccepting parent. The adaptation chosen is a personal response; infants in like circumstances make different choices. The adaptation Compensatory Responses is illustrated in Chapter 7, "Some Choose Sides, and Some Choose Success," and in Chapter 8, "Male and Female."

The Value of Adaptations

The above adaptations provide the unborn infant with a means of dealing with the stress she feels in the womb environment. When the stress seems extreme, her responses might be called "survival" adaptations.

The adaptations we make often strongly motivate us, after birth, to develop skills and abilities that are highly beneficial to us. For example, the determination to succeed—a compensatory adaptation—is likely to lead a person to develop qualities such as persistence, self-reliance, mental acuity, and expressiveness.

We reach a point in our lives when we outgrow our patterns and are ready to expand beyond the limitations of a particular adaptation and life orientation. When our adaptation has led us to develop positive qualities, a smooth transition into a new way of functioning is more likely.

When we have developed negative qualities, we are sometimes pressured to change because of unhappiness. Let me provide an example of this. An infant in the womb makes an adaptation to withdraw from the emotional energies of life (adaptation

#3, above). She establishes a way of functioning that allows her to feel safe and in control of her life. Having removed herself from the currents of life, she may later in life feel lonely and isolated; life may feel meaningless. When her life becomes unpleasant enough, or a vision of a happier life becomes enticing, she may be impelled to expand beyond those limitations. A new phase of her development will begin.

Soul Perspective

The adaptation that an infant makes depends on her innate character, that is, a genetic or constitutional propensity toward certain kinds of responses. As we strive to overcome the limitations that result from our adaptations, we develop desirable personal qualities: effectiveness of action, personal power, creativity, the ability to communicate, love of others, empathy, awareness, understanding, etc. From a soul perspective, all of our experiences, including difficult prenatal experiences, are prompted by our deeper purpose in being here, our personal evolution. Our adversity encourages us to develop those skills that enable us to achieve happiness, fulfillment, and self-realization.

Appendix C

Processes for Releasing Prenatal Stress and Trauma

I use four steps for resolving prenatal wounds: 1. Recall, 2. Reframing, 3. Releasing, and 4. Rescripting. It may take a number of sessions to complete the healing process. I use hypnosis as a primary technique for regressing my clients to their prenatal experiences When the therapy is accomplished, these prenatal experiences are, for the adult, a source of energizing feelings. Emotional limitations have lifted, and the potential for greater personal fulfillment has increased. The four steps are described below.

Recall of Affecting Experiences

In this process, the adult client examines her early life experiences, including prebirth and birth experiences. This review brings out of obscurity the hidden, but highly influential, formative experiences. It gives words to experiences for which the infant could have no words, allowing those experiences to be clearly recognized, understood, and evaluated by the adult mind.

Reframing: Educating the Infant Within

Reframing means that events are reinterpreted by applying adult insight and understanding. The regression process educates the adult so that she has a more complete view of the family dynamic. She develops a more accurate understanding of the motives, psychology, and interactions of her family members.

In regression, the adult self speaks to and forms a relationship with the emotionally-centered prenatal infant self. The adult's ability to convey logical information to the infant is limited, just as it would be in trying to educate a four-year-old child to understand the meaning of a divorce. However, the presence, energy, feelings, and understanding of the adult can strongly affect the prenatal infant self, opening the door to an effective resolution of the infant's emotional distress.

Releasing the Assumed Emotions

Putting emotions into words helps to release them. Reliving and understanding our early experiences releases anger, protectiveness, hostility, vulnerability, hurt, inadequacy, and blame. We become more neutral and give up emotional alliances and attachments. The statement "the truth shall make you free" is more than a truism. Hypnotic regression offers a deep, clear, intensely felt reliving of early experiences, leading to a deep level of emotional release.

Rescripting

With the release of the limiting emotional biases, the client becomes free to reexperience her history in the light of a new, more adult perception of the situation, and to build a new personal psychology. *Rescripting allows the emotional patterns to be restructured.* The client is provided with alternative responses to the pattern that has been repeated throughout her life.

Specific Rescripting Techniques

Rescripting processes can be healing, leading to more effective modes of behavior. Active imagination and mental imagery are used to imprint a new, positive image of the prebirth experience. A different core feeling and emotional tone are established to replace the negative qualities of the original experience. These techniques elicit our inner potential for wholeness and integration and draw forth a more affirmative, life-giving energy. Below are brief explanations of techniques I have found useful.

1. Experiencing the gestation as the child of "ideal parents."

The infant is given the experience of being free of the original parents. Rather, she experiences her gestation surrounded in love, nurtured, and validated by "ideal" parents—parents who fully appreciate and support her. She experiences each month of the gestation, then matures through childhood, adolescence, and adulthood, in a positive interaction with them. I find that virtually all clients are able to experience how it feels to have a supportive environment and to live in a more vital way. The client is given the opportunity to feel trustful, open, adventuresome, valued, and loved by others. She experiences a positive sense of life and relationships that serve as a model for her development.

2. Experiencing the gestation with the underlying love the parents held for their unborn infant and for each other fully expressed.

Though parents love their infants, they often fail to express the full measure of their love. Psychological limitations, such as fear, hurt, a sense of unworthiness, and strict ideals about how life should be lived, often limit the way parents express their love for each other and for their infant. This rescripting process is designed to bypass such limitations. In this process the parents and children live out the true, often powerful, underlying love within the family—the love that created the marriage and family. This enables the infant to feel that she is part of a loving family. The infant, more in touch with the truth, is prepared to experience the environment of the womb as nurturing. I find that some clients are more open to this experience after they have healed some of their hurt through the process of "ideal parents."

3. Separating from the parents' identity and emotions.

This process—quite the opposite of the one just described—is used to "rescue" the prenatal infant from parents who feel ill-willed toward their infant. The client cuts the psychic cords to her parents. This allows her to recognize and claim herself as a separate identity with her own intrinsic qualities and potential. In this process she visualizes and experiences in detail her growth and maturation.

4. Reliving the prenatal experience while accompanied by one's own adult self, a friend, or a spiritual guide.

In the therapeutic process of "Healing the Child Within," the child is guided through the early life experiences by the more mature and knowledgeable adult self. The adult self speaks to the prenatal infant self still present within, and they live out a relationship of a child supported by an empathetic, loving adult. This allows the infant to feel a constant supportive presence, and to experience the benefits of developing in a more secure environment. The infant matures through the stages of life with the feeling of support that she experiences with this loving adult influence.

Those who have done so find that the "infant within" is a psychic entity with her own ways of responding and her own pattern of development. The infant within, in her relationship with the caring adult, is just as spontaneous and unpredictable as a living infant would be. Characteristically, as the relationship continues, the infant within no longer feels isolated, but rather feels safe enough to fully express herself.

In a variation of this process, the infant allies with a "friend" or a guardian angel or guide, rather than with the adult self. This variation is useful when my client is so identified with her child self, and has so little confidence in her own adult functions, that she is not able to be effective in an adult role.

5. Reliving the prenatal experience from the level of one's own spiritual identity.

This can be done by bringing into the womb the light and energy of the spiritual dimension in which we live before incarnating, where we experience wholeness, peace, and unity. Keeping the consciousness of a spiritual home allows some of my clients to feel less vulnerable while reliving the gestation.

A slightly different process may be used which brings the client back to the point of being a spirit that has not yet taken a body, and then reliving the prenatal experience with an awareness of being this spirit. This allows the client to maintain the connection with the spiritual self, and to keep an awareness of her intrinsic identity.

6. Bringing light energy into the wounded area of one's self.

This process involves bringing healing light into the area of one's being that feels wounded or weak. This wound may be experienced as emotional, physical or psychic. It can be sensed even though, like emotions, it may not be directly identified as part of the physical body.

Effectiveness of Rescripting

As therapists, we assist our clients in releasing the constraints of fear, guilt, anger, blame, poor self-esteem, and excessive responsibility so that they may express their potential for love and creative expression. Our fundamental life energy seeks to be expressed, seeks to overcome constraints and limitations.

The rescripting process allows the client to vividly experience, through active imagination, the things she most deeply desires. Through *repetition* of the new way of expression, the new pattern is deepened and is eventually outwardly expressed.

Rescripting is an effective technique because it releases our underlying energies. It transcends the limitations of our personal psychology to express the longing of our spirit: we desire to harmoniously engage with those with whom we have a soul connection, those we love and who are precious to us.

Psychological illness is often the result of deprivation. By expressing a higher level of spiritual truth and union, healing may come about. We seek to allow the power of who we are as souls and spirits to hold greater sway in our lives, to manifest with a more brilliant light. We strive to be in our physical form the radiant spirits and immortal beings we truly are.

Bibliography

Chamberlain, David, Ph.D. *Babies Remember Birth.* Los Angeles: Jeremy P. Tarcher, 1988.

Presents scientific and medical evidence regarding preborn and newborn infants, as well as case studies of birth memories obtained under hypnosis.

Church, Dawson. *Communing With the Spirit of Your Unborn Child.* San Leandro, CA: Aslan Publishing, 1988.

A clear "how to" manual for parents who wish to explore pregnancy, birth, and infancy from a spiritual perspective.

English, Jane Butterfield. *Different Doorway: Adventures of a Caesarean Born.* Point Reyes Station, CA: Earth Heart, 1985.

A record of the author's intensive self-exploration into how her birth—a non-labor caesarean section—affected her life.

Grof, Stanislav, M.D., Ph.D. *Beyond the Brain: Birth, Death, and Transcendence in Psychotherapy.* Albany, NY: State University of New York Press, 1985.

Visionary work by an influential research psychologist and leader in the transpersonal psychology movement. Includes discussion on perinatal experience and fetal consciousness. Correlates birth traumas with effects upon later life personality. This book is currently out of print.

Grof, Stanislav, M.D., Ph.D., and Bennett, Hal Zina, Ph.D. *The Holotropic Mind: Three Levels of Human Consciousness and How They Shape Our Lives.* San Francisco: Harpers San Francisco, 1992.

Presents a new understanding of human nature and development that incorporates experiences before, during, and immediately after birth, as well as other spiritual realms.

Janov, Arthur, Ph.D. *Imprints: The Lifelong Effects of the Birth Experience.* New York: Coward-McCann, 1983.

Explores the use of primal therapy to relive birth trauma and to release behavior unconsciously based on birth memory. This book is currently out of print.

Landsman, Sandra G., Ph.D. *Found: A Place for Me.* Farmington Hills, MI: Treehouse Enterprises, 1984.

A psychotherapist traces the roots of manic-depressive disorders to experiences in the womb.

Leboyer, Frederick, M.D. *Birth Without Violence.* New York: Alfred A. Knopf, 1976.

Poetic and powerful plea to make birth an easier experience for the vulnerable, sensitive newborn.

Monroe, Robert A., *Journeys Out of the Body*. New York: Doubleday & Co., 1973.

This book describes the experiences associated with "astral travel"—when consciousness travels out of the physical body.

Moody, Raymond A. Jr., M.D. *Life After Life*. New York: Bantam Books, 1975.

This book investigates stories of people who have experienced "clinical death" and later been revived. Reports of their experiences provide evidence of the survival of the human soul beyond death.

Ray, Sondra, and Mandel,Bob. *Birth and Relationships: How Your Birth Affects Your Relationships*. Berkeley, CA: Celestial Arts, 1987.

Case studies illustrating the connection between different types of birth and later relationships and life patterns, presented by two leaders of the rebirthing movement.

Verny, Thomas, M.D., with Kelly, John . *The Secret Life of the Unborn Child*. New York: Dell, 1981.

Makes accessible the research findings of the past two decades regarding unborn infants and newborns, revealing how parents can contribute, even before birth, to the well-being of their children. A pioneer work.

Verny, Thomas, M.D., and Weintraub, Pamela. *Nurturing the Unborn Child*. New York: Bantam Doubleday Dell, 1991.

Provides prospective parents with a well developed and organized program enabling them to create a nurturing relationship with their infant in utero.

Wambach, Helen, Ph.D. *Life Before Life*. New York: Bantam Books, 1979.

Presents a psychologist's research findings of 750 subjects who, using hypnosis, explored their experiences before birth.

Other Resources

Pre and Peri-Natal Psychology Association of North America (PPPANA). 2162 Ingleside Avenue, Macon, GA 31204.

Michael Gabriel, P.O. Box 8030, San Jose, CA 95155–8030

Other Books from Aslan Publishing

Facing Death, Finding Love
by Dawson Church
This is the searingly honest account of the death of a baby, and of a father's struggle to come to terms with the finality of his loss. The author deals honestly with the endless round of medical procedures, anguished relatives and stunned friends. Without melodrama or self-pity, he relates how it felt to have a memorial service for a life that never saw the light of day. In the end, this is a book about tragedy that refuses to wallow in tragedy, but finds instead a bedrock of life-affirming joy.

$10.95

Gentle Roads to Survival
by Andre Auw, Ph.D.
Psychologist Andre Auw, a close associate of the great 20th-century psychologists Carl Rogers and Virginia Satir, characterizes people who learn to prevail over life's challenges as survivors. Using dozens of case histories, poems, and allegories, Auw identifies the lessons all survivors know: characteristics that distinguish people who give up hope from those who find the inspiration and encouragement to carry on.

$9.95

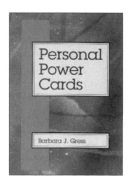

Personal Power Cards
by Barbara Gress
A simple, easy to use set of flash cards for emotional wellness. Includes 55 cards, a carrying pouch, and an 80 page booklet. The Cards help retrain your feelings to be positive and healthy. Their combination of colors, shapes, and words allow positive thoughts to penetrate deep into your subconscious, "programming" your emotions for health.

$18.95

Living at the Heart of Creation
by Michael Exeter
Living at the Heart of Creation is not a self-help manual or a "fix-it" book of superficial answers. It is, rather, an intelligent yet simple offering of insight into such challenging areas as the environmental crises, overpopulation, business relationships, and personal well-being. Michael Exeter shows exactly what it means to live at the heart of creation—to live at the place T. S. Eliot called "the still point of the turning world." This book will be a friend and companion to anyone with the desire to explore what it means to be vibrant and wise in these extraordinary times.

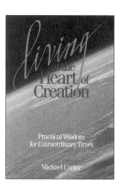

$9.95

Other Books from Aslan Publishing

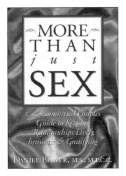

More Than Just Sex
by Daniel Beaver, M.S., M.F.C.C.
While our generation is freer than ever before to explore and experiment with sex, our superficial liberation masks a chronic sense of failure and anxiety about unfulfilling sexual experiences. A relationships counselor with over eighteen years of experience in counseling a wide variety of relationship problems, Dan Beaver, MFCC, brings together a depth and breadth of authoritative information not previously available from a single source.

$12.95

When You See a Sacred Cow… Milk It for All It's Worth!
by Swami Beyondananda
The "Yogi from Muskogee" is at it again. In this delightful, off-the-wall little book, Swami Beyondananda holds forth on the ozone layer, Porky Pig, Safe Sects, and the theology of Chocolate. Read a few lines and you'll quickly realize that nothing's safe from his pointblank scrutiny.

$9.95

Winds Across the Sky
by Chris Foster
Every so often a novel comes along that is simple, magical, utterly unique and compelling. Winds Across the Sky is that kind of rare, exceptional work. Woven around the themes of ecology, recovery, male-female relationships, and other great issues of the day, Chris Foster's lean prose and poetic style make this a book that pierces the heart of the reader. This book portrays the fundamental unity of all creation in a new way and across a broader spectrum. It portrays loving communication as it occurs easily between different species and between humans and the natural world.

$9.95

Your Body Believes Every Word You Say
by Barbara Hoberman Levine
This bestselling title describes the link between language and disease. Levine's fifteen-year battle with a huge brain tumor led her to trace common words and phrases like "that breaks my heart" and "it's a pain in the butt" back to the underlying beliefs on which they are based and the symptoms they cause. With over 30,000 copies in print, this book is on it's way to becoming one of the classics of modern healing literature.

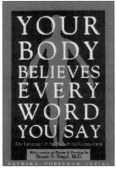

$11.95

Order Form

Date _____

Name _____

Address _____

City _____ State_____ Zip _____

Phone _____

Please send a catalog to my friend:

Name _____

Address _____

_____

Item	Qty.	Price	Amount
Facing Death, Finding Love		$10.95	
Gentle Roads to Survival		$9.95	
Personal Power Cards		$18.95	
Living at the Heart of Creation		$9.95	
More Than Just Sex		$12.95	
When You See a Sacred Cow…		$9.95	
Winds Across the Sky		$9.95	
Your Body Believes Every Word You Say		$11.95	

	Subtotal	
Calif. res. add 7.5%	Sales Tax	
	Shipping	
	Grand Total	

Add for shipping:
Book Rate: $2.50 for first item, $1.00 for ea. add. item.
First Class/UPS: $4.00 for first item, $1.50 ea. add. item.
Canada/Mexico: One-and-a-half times shipping rates.
Overseas: Double shipping rates.

Check type of payment:

☐ Check or money order enclosed

☐ Visa ☐ MasterCard

Acct. # _____

Exp. Date _____

Signature _____

Send order to:
**Aslan Publishing
3356 Coffey Lane
Santa Rosa, CA 95403**
or call to order:
(800) 275-2606

MNN